Hallmarks of Design

Evidence of purposeful design and beauty in nature

Stuart Burgess

DayOne

© Day One Publications 2000
First printed 2000
Revised Edition 2002

Scripture quotations are from The New King James Version
© 1982 Thomas Nelson Inc.

British Library Cataloguing in Publication Data available
ISBN 1 903087 31 7

Published by Day One Publications
3 Epsom Business Park, Kiln Lane, Epsom, Surrey KT17 1JF
☎ 01372 728 300 FAX 01372 722 400
email—sales@dayone.co.uk
www.dayone.co.uk

Designed by Steve Devane and printed by CPD

Dedication
This book is dedicated to my wife Jocelyn
and our children: Samuel, Naomi, Keziah,
Tabitha and Josiah.

Acknowledgements

I received many comments on the first edition and the draft of the second edition for which I am very grateful. I am especially thankful to Nancy Darrall, David Tyler, Sheena Tyler, Philip Bell and David Sherwood. I am also very grateful to my wife Jocelyn for doing another excellent editing job with the grammar and style.

Stuart Burgess
May 2002
Department of Mechanical Engineering
Queen's Building, University Walk
University of Bristol
BS8 1TR

Contents

Preface

It gives me great pleasure to write a foreword to this excellent book *Hallmarks of Design*. From his experience in various aspects of design in engineering, Dr Burgess is well qualified to bring his expertise to bear on the subject of design in nature. I have always contended that the evidence for design in nature invalidates any theory of evolution and this book, particularly its consideration of the presence of 'complete optimum design', strongly supports this conviction.

I well remember, as a student of zoology, being faced with the teaching of evolution in a zoology course and the conflict this caused in my thinking until I recalled a biblical truth, 'By faith we understand that the worlds were framed by the word of God' (Hebrews 11:3). This helped me at the time but later, from my reading in philosophy and a lifetime of experimental science, I realised that 'Christian faith' was not a 'blind leap in the dark' but was founded on factual evidence. For instance, the second law of thermodynamics, the decay of radioactive molecules and the impossibility that complex structures in the plant and animal kingdom could be produced by thousands of minute gradual steps of ever increasing complexity over millions of years, militated against the theory of evolution.

Evolution is a man-made 'theory' to explain the origin and continuance of life on this planet without reference to a Creator. For instance, Sir Julian Huxley in *'Evolution: a modern synthesis'* wrote, 'Modern science must rule out special creation or divine guidance'. But why? Science, by its conscious elimination of questions of final cause and purpose from its deductions, can never claim to be the only means of apprehending human experience and knowledge. Any theory must embrace the 'whole man' including feelings, emotions, pleasure, beauty, morals, motives, final cause and purpose and, not least, life after death.

It is my firm conviction that the Christian faith is no flimsy idea but a reality born of experience which bears no other interpretation. It is my earnest wish and prayer that this book will lead its readers to the same conclusion.

Alan Linton, PhD, DSc, FRCPath., Hon. Assoc. RCVS
Emeritus Professor of Bacteriology
Formerly Head of Department of Microbiology, Bristol University

E ver since William Paley used 'design in nature' to argue for the existence of the Great Designer, there has been fierce denial of such arguments. Possibly some may have been impressed by the fine language but left dissatisfied by the tortuous logic of *The Blind Watchmaker* and other books by Professor Richard Dawkins. How refreshing that in this book, *Hallmarks of Design*, Dr Stuart Burgess writes in plain, easy-to-understand terms of the complexity and beauty of living creatures all around us. He argues, with great insight from his expertise in mechanical engineering, that the interrelation of intricate mechanisms can make sense only by recognising that, just like cars and planes, living creatures are designed.

Paley's argument from design in living creatures is in fact far from dead. Rather it is stronger than ever, and is very much at the forefront of the creation/evolution debate. The reason for this is that the argument concerning purposeful design in the world and universe is readily understood by young and old alike, whether scientifically trained or otherwise. Not only that, but the design argument is scriptural and powerful. We are created to appreciate design, order, pattern and beauty. If we choose to ignore this, we do so at our eternal peril. The Apostle Paul teaches (Romans 1:20) that the invisible things of Him are clearly seen, being understood by the things that are made, even His eternal power and Godhead; so that they are without excuse. God has placed His hallmark on creation, and it is this argument that Dr Stuart Burgess brilliantly expounds. Readers of this book will be intrigued by the delightful summary of example after example, showing the hallmarks of design in the natural world, and they will want to bring many of the well laid-out facts of this book into conversation with friends and neighbours. Armed with this material, many scientists and non-scientists alike will, by God's grace, have their eyes opened as to the shallowness of evolutionary philosophy. May many see that the argument from design shouts powerfully of the Creator who spans the Heavens, and yet stooped to become Man, in order to be our Saviour.

Andy C. McIntosh, DSc, FIMA, CMath, FInstE, CEng
Professor of Combustion Theory
Department of Fuel & Energy, The University of Leeds

The Design Argument argues that design reveals a designer and the attributes of the designer. The Design Argument is very important because design provides positive evidence for a Creator and not just evidence against evolution. Following modern discoveries of the staggering complexity and beauty of nature, the Design Argument is stronger than ever before.

I have presented the Design Argument by concentrating on hallmarks of intelligent design. The supposed process of evolution is inherently severely limited in the amount of order that it could produce because of the huge restrictions of incremental change and natural selection. In contrast, an intelligent designer has no such restrictions and can create extreme levels of order, beauty and purpose. This book describes six *hallmarks of design* that can only be produced by an intelligent designer:

1 Irreducible mechanisms
2 Complete optimum design
3 Added beauty
4 Extreme similarity in features
5 Extreme diversity of kinds
6 Man-centred features

At the beginning of each chapter I describe how these are important and common hallmarks of intelligent design in engineering. Each chapter then describes how the hallmarks are very clearly seen in nature. I also explain how nature contains a far superior level of design than man-made design.

I have concentrated on mechanical (macro) design rather than biochemical (micro) design in nature because this is my field of expertise. One advantage of macro design is that it is more familiar and understandable to the general reader. Macro design also has the advantage that it includes the hallmarks of added beauty and man-centred features. These hallmarks are not so relevant at the biochemical level.

I have not tried to argue that organisms are unchanging from one generation to the next. A particular kind of creature such as the dog kind has great genetic potential and this has produced a great variety of dogs over the course of history. What I have argued is that there are such profound differences between the different kinds of organisms in nature that they cannot have evolved from a common ancestor. I also have not tried to argue that nature is perfect and beautiful in every respect. Nature has been affected by the Fall of Adam and Eve in the Garden of Eden and this has produced undesirable aspects such as disease, violence and death. However, despite these blemishes, there is still clear evidence of design in nature.

Note on second edition

The whole book has been completely revised in this second edition. There are three new chapters on the subject of beauty: the beauty of the peacock tail, the beauty of bird song and the beauty of the human body. Beauty has not been used much before as evidence of design. However, in engineering and architecture it is well known that beauty is a very important hallmark of design. In addition, modern research has shown that the human being has a real capacity for appreciating beauty. For example, it has been found that the human brain has specific areas which are dedicated to appreciating beauty in music. It is very difficult to think of any evolutionary reason why the human brain should have the ability to appreciate music since this gives no survival advantage. I believe that the beauty of nature and man's ability to appreciate that beauty presents one of the biggest challenges to the atheist and one of the biggest encouragements to the believer.

The issue of origins is very important because it greatly affects the answers to other ultimate questions such as the purpose of life and what happens after death. Considering the importance of origins, it is very important to be aware of the evidence for a Creator rather than just blindly accepting the theory of evolution. I hope that this book encourages many people by showing that there is overwhelming and positive evidence for a loving Creator.

Irreducible mechanisms: The irreducible knee joint

Then God said, 'Let the earth bring forth the living creature according to its kind: cattle and creeping thing and beast of the earth, each according to its kind'; and it was so (Genesis 1:24).

T he Bible teaches that all the different kinds of creature in nature have been directly created by God and have not evolved from a common primitive ancestor. For example, the verse above from Genesis 1 describes how God created different 'kinds' of land creature on the sixth day of creation. Examples of kinds include the horse, cow, dog and cat. Irreducible mechanisms like the mammalian knee joint[1] provide powerful living evidence that creatures were indeed created as distinct kinds.

1.1 Hallmark of design: irreducible mechanisms

An irreducible mechanism is a mechanism that must have several parts simultaneously present and assembled to perform a useful function. In addition, each part usually has several essential characteristics. A mechanical watch is an example of an irreducible mechanism because it requires several separate parts such as gears, spring and clock hands to function. Also, each of these parts has several essential characteristics such as gear teeth and connecting holes. If a mechanical watch is missing an essential part like the spring, then it cannot perform any useful function. Also, if one of the essential details of one of these parts is missing such as a connection between a gear and a shaft, then the watch cannot function.

An irreducible mechanism can only be created by an intelligent designer because only an intelligent designer can plan ahead and design all the parts and characteristics simultaneously. An irreducible mechanism cannot be produced by a process of evolution because evolution is limited to incremental change. The existence of an irreducible mechanism provides powerful evidence for intelligent design whether the mechanism is man-made or natural.

It is important to realise that evolutionists fully agree that evolution cannot produce irreducible mechanisms. For example, in his *Origin of Species*, Charles Darwin said:

> If it could be demonstrated that any complex organ existed which could not possibly have been formed by numerous, successive, slight modifications, my theory would absolutely break down.[2]

Modern-day evolutionists also agree that evolution cannot produce irreducible mechanisms.[3] Like Darwin, modern-day evolutionists believe that there are no irreducible mechanisms in nature and that every mechanism in nature has evolved by 'numerous, successive, slight modifications'. However, there is tremendous evidence that there are many irreducible mechanisms in nature both at a macro (mechanical) level and at a micro (biochemical) level.[4] This chapter shows that the mammalian knee joint is a clear example of a mechanical mechanism that could not have evolved. Chapters 2 and 3 will give other examples of irreducible mechanisms in nature.

1.2 The mammalian knee joint

The main types of limb joint in mammals are the ball and socket joint (hip and shoulder) and the hinge joint (elbow and knee). The main function of the knee joint is to form a hinge between the lower leg and the upper leg. The majority of biology textbooks describe the knee joint just as a 'hinge', giving the impression that there is just a simple pivot between the upper and lower leg bones. However, this is a gross over-simplification because the knee joint is actually a very sophisticated mechanism and a masterpiece of design.

A schematic of the knee joint is shown in Figs. 1–1 and 1–2. The pictures show a human knee, although it should be noted that many animal knees have a similar basic structure. The knee is called a condylar joint[5] because of the rolling and sliding action (articulation) between the upper leg bone (the femur) and the main lower leg bone (the tibia). The femur bone has two protrusions (called condyles) and these have a convex curvature in order to

Rolling and sliding

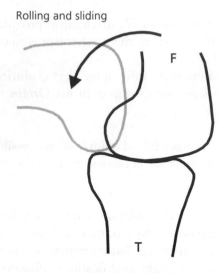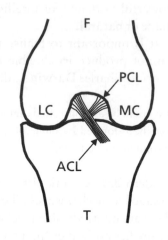

(a) Side view of knee   **(b)** Front view of knee

F   Femur
T   Tibia
LC Lateral condyle
MC Medial condyle
PCL Posterior cruciate ligament
ACL Anterior cruciate ligament

Fig. 1–1 Anatomy of the knee joint (peripheral ligaments and knee cap removed)

roll and slide against the tibia bone. The tibia bone has two concave grooves which match the condyles of the femur bone. The two central ligaments which connect the tibia to the femur are called cruciate ligaments because of the way they form a cross. The cruciate ligaments fit neatly inside the space between the two condyles. The main function of the cruciate ligaments is to guide the motion of the knee joint.

The two cruciate ligaments and the two leg bones form a very sophisticated and precise mechanism, called a 'four-bar mechanism'.[6] The four-bar mechanism of the knee is shown at various stages of rotation in Fig. 1–2. These stages of rotation are schematically presented in Fig. 1–3 to show clearly how the four-bar mechanism produces a hinge movement. The

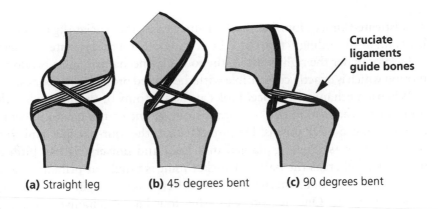

(a) Straight leg **(b)** 45 degrees bent **(c)** 90 degrees bent

Cruciate ligaments guide bones

Fig. 1–2 The irreducible mechanism of the knee (bones cut to show ligaments)

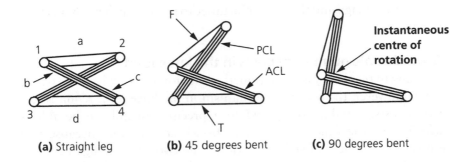

(a) Straight leg **(b)** 45 degrees bent **(c)** 90 degrees bent

Instantaneous centre of rotation

Fig. 1–3 Schematic of the four-bar mechanism in the knee joint

cruciate ligaments form the two crossed bars (b & c) whilst the upper and lower bones form the other two bars (a & d). The cruciate ligaments are able to pivot where they are attached to the bones (points 1, 2, 3 & 4) because they are made of a flexible material. In a four-bar mechanism, the length of each of the four bars remains approximately constant but the angle between each bar can change in order for the upper and lower bars to rotate relative to each other.

One important feature of the four-bar mechanism is that it does not have a fixed point of rotation as does a pivot hinge. The knee joint is a particularly sophisticated kind of four-bar mechanism because the cruciate ligaments are kept taut by the rolling action of the bones. In order for the cruciate ligaments to be kept under the right tension, the four-bar mechanism must produce a motion which is exactly compatible with the curved profile of the bones.

When a mechanical engineer looks at the anatomy of the human leg, the four-bar mechanism in the knee stands out as one of the most important and impressive mechanisms. Despite this fact, the four-bar mechanism in the knee joint is rarely explained in school and university-level biology textbooks. Whereas the ball and socket joint is taught at primary school level, the four-bar mechanism is often not taught to biology undergraduates. One reason why the four-bar mechanism is rarely mentioned in biology textbooks could be that the authors do not understand mechanical mechanisms. However, it is also possible that the authors realise that sophisticated mechanical mechanisms bear the hallmarks of design and there is a reluctance to present such mechanisms to students.

1.3 Irreducible number of parts in the knee joint

According to the theory of evolution, the knee joint has evolved one part at a time. However, the four-bar mechanism in the knee joint requires four parts to exist simultaneously and in a precise assembly to be able to perform its basic function. The two bones are essential because they perform the rolling and sliding motion. The two cruciate ligaments are essential because they perform a vital guiding function in the joint, as shown in Fig. 1–2. The four parts are interdependent with each other and must always exist together to be of any use. If just one cruciate ligament is removed, then the joint cannot function as a hinge and the joint has no other useful function.

The importance of having all the parts of the four-bar mechanism in place simultaneously is demonstrated by the serious nature of knee injuries. When a cruciate ligament is snapped, the knee cannot function unless major surgery is carried out to repair the ligament. The fact that the mammalian knee requires a minimum of four complex parts provides powerful evidence that it did not evolve and that it was created as a fully functioning mechanism on the sixth day of creation.

1.4 Irreducible number of characteristics in the knee joint

The four essential parts of the knee joint also contain an irreducible number of 'essential characteristics'. According to evolution, all the characteristics of the knee have evolved one at a time. However, there are at least 16 essential characteristics in the knee joint, as shown in Table 1–1. It could be argued that the knee joint also requires characteristics to describe the leg muscles that are needed to make the joint move. However, these have been left out because the evolutionist might argue that these happened to exist in some 'primitive joint'. Therefore, the 16 characteristics represent a conservative estimate of the minimum required characteristics in the knee joint.

If one of the characteristics shown in Table 1–1 is missing, then the knee cannot function at all. The 16 characteristics must not only be present but must also be precisely compatible with each other in order to produce the right physical motion. The two bones must have a compatible curvature at their interface and this curvature must also be precisely compatible with the motion produced by the cruciate ligaments. If the attachment points are not in the right place on the bones, then the motion of the four-bar mechanism will not be compatible with the rolling motion of the bones, and the knee will seize up or fall apart. The ligaments must also be assembled to the correct attachment points so that the ligaments form a cross, as shown in Fig. 1–2. If one of the ligaments is assembled to the wrong attachment point, then the four-bar mechanism cannot work and the knee cannot function as a hinge.

Table 1–1 Essential characteristics in the knee joint

PART	ESSENTIAL CHARACTERISTICS	No. OF CHARACTERISTICS
Femur bone	Protrusion of two condyles	2
	Convex curvature of two condyles	2
	Position of ligament attachment points 1& 2	2
Tibia bone	Concave curvature of two tracks	2
	Position of ligament attachment points 3 & 4	2
Anterior cruciate ligament	Assembly of ligament to points 1 & 4	2
	Length of ligament	1
Posterior cruciate ligament	Assembly of ligament to points 2 & 3	2
	Length of ligament	1
	TOTAL	16

1.5 Irreducible amount of information in the genetic code

THE GENETIC CODE

In order for the parts of a mechanism to be manufactured and assembled, it is necessary for there to be a set of instructions that specify all the characteristics of each part. Table 1–2 below summarises how information about characteristics is specified in living organisms and engineering. The table shows that there is an analogy between the information in the genetic code of organisms and the information in the engineering drawings of a man-made machine.

Table 1–2 Information in living organisms and engineering

GENETIC CODE	ENGINEERING DRAWINGS
Set of chromosomes (genetic code)	Set of drawings
Individual chromosome	Subset of drawings
String of chemical units (gene)	Paragraph of writing (characteristic)
One chemical unit (base pair)	One letter

In the case of a man-made mechanism like a watch, the characteristics of the parts are described on a set of drawings. Individual parts are shown on individual drawings and individual characteristics are described by paragraphs on the drawings. For example, a gear would usually be described on one drawing and there would be several paragraphs describing characteristics of the gear such as diameter, thickness, tooth shape and material. The accuracy of design information in engineering is very important. An error in just one letter of a paragraph could produce a fault in a part which could prevent the watch from working.

In the case of living organisms, the characteristics of the organism such as eye colour are specified by information in the genetic code. The genetic code is analogous to a complete set of engineering drawings and a copy of the genetic code is found in the nucleus of every cell in the body. An adult human has many trillions of cells and thus many trillions of copies of the genetic code in the body!

The genetic code is written on a tiny molecule called DNA. The DNA of a human being has 46 separate sections called chromosomes. DNA contains information in the form of a very long sequence of chemical 'letters'. There are four different chemical letters and the sequence of these letters produces information in a way which is analogous to Morse code. (The four chemical 'letters' are nucleotide molecules: adenylic acid (A), thymidylic acid (T), cytidylic acid (C), and guanylic acid (G)). DNA has a double helix structure and each helix contains its own string of chemical letters. The letters from each helix line up with each other exactly and are joined together to form base pairs. One reason why DNA has a double helical structure is that it enables the DNA to divide into two parts when a cell divides, allowing a perfect copy of DNA to appear in both cells.

A chromosome contains the information of many physical characteristics and is analogous to a subset of drawings. Even though each chromosome contains a long continuous series of chemical letters, this long list can be divided up into groups of letters called genes. A gene typically consists of several hundred chemical units of information and it is the genes which largely determine the characteristics of an organism. A typical function of the genes is to specify different types of proteins which are needed by the organism to grow and function. A gene is analogous to a paragraph on an engineering drawing and the chemical units in a gene are analogous to the letters in a paragraph. A living organism is continually reading instructions from DNA in order to carry out life's processes such as growth and repair. Organisms such as mammals typically have many thousands of genes and millions of chemical letters in their genetic code.

IRREDUCIBLE AMOUNT OF INFORMATION

Evolutionists believe that information in the genetic code has evolved one unit at a time. However, the knee joint has at least 16 essential characteristics and this requires the simultaneous presence of a great deal of information. At present, scientists do not know how geometrical characteristics, such as ligament attachment points, are specified by the body. However, there must be information somewhere which specifies such critical characteristics. If it is assumed that each characteristic requires at least the same amount of information as that required to specify one gene (say 1000 chemical units), then many thousand units of information would be required to be simultaneously present for the knee to work. These chemical units represent an irreducible amount of information in the genetic code.

Not only must all the genetic information be present from the start but it must also remain unchanged. In the case of a healthy knee joint, if a random change occurs to the information which specifies one of the essential characteristics, such as the position of a ligament, then the knee will cease to function properly.

1.6 Uniqueness of the knee joint

The knee is a unique type of joint because it uses completely different mechanical principles to those used by other joints in the body. Whereas the knee has two ligaments that perform a vital guidance role (the cruciate ligaments), the joints of the hip, shoulder and elbow have no such ligaments at all. Whereas the knee rolls and slides, the joints of the hip, shoulder and elbow only slide. Whereas the knee has a centre of rotation that moves by up to several centimetres, the joints of the hip, shoulder and elbow have a fixed centre of rotation. Indeed, a pivot hinge has none of the characteristics shown in Table 1–1. In particular, a pivot joint has nothing remotely like the two crossed cruciate ligaments at the centre of the joint.

Advanced textbooks on anatomy sometimes acknowledge that the mammalian knee joint is a unique type of joint.[7] However, these books never attempt to explain how the knee could have evolved. It is very difficult to explain how an evolutionary process could cause two ligaments to suddenly become crossed at the centre of a pivot joint precisely at the same time that a space is formed to accommodate them and precisely at the same time that a complex and compatible rolling motion is produced!

If the knee joint had evolved, one would fully expect to find many intermediate forms of joint between the pivot joint (elbow) and the knee joint either in living creatures or extinct creatures. However, there is absolutely no evidence that any intermediate form of joint has ever existed. Considering the large number of fossils that have been studied and considering that no intermediate forms of joint have been found between a pivot joint and a knee joint, it must be concluded that there is overwhelming evidence that the knee has not evolved.

If the knee joint had evolved, it should at the very least be possible to 'imagine' what intermediate forms of joint should look like. Considering the ingenuity of man, this should not be a difficult task if intermediate forms are possible. However, all attempts to imagine intermediate forms of knee joint have failed. The failure to imagine intermediate forms of mechanisms throughout the animal kingdom has been fully acknowledged by leading evolutionists such as Stephen Jay Gould who has said:

Our inability, even in our imagination, to construct functional intermediates in many cases has been a persistent and nagging problem for gradualistic accounts of evolution.[8]

1.7 Growth of the knee joint

The fact that the knee joint must be grown in the developing embryo adds further complexity to the design. As well as specifying all the characteristics of the knee joint, the cell must also specify how the knee will grow and become assembled. The knee joint is formed in the early part of pregnancy, within about 12 weeks of conception. In the early weeks of life, the human embryo has limb buds where the legs and arms will develop, as shown in Fig. 1–4. Each of the cells in each limb bud contains all the information necessary to construct the limb. The cell not only specifies the materials of the ligaments, muscles and bones but it also has the amazing ability to specify the positioning and timing information which is necessary to assemble these parts.

When each leg limb bud reaches a certain size, instructions are somehow given for the bone in the limb bud to separate and form the separate bones of the lower and upper leg. Instructions are also somehow given for the cruciate ligaments to form a cross and connect with the bones to make an assembled knee joint. The positioning and timing of the ligament connections and the splitting of the leg bones must take place with great precision in order for the knee joint to be produced. The self-assembly of the knee joint is so sophisticated that scientists do not know how it happens. A recent textbook on the development of organisms says:

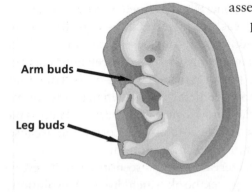

Arm buds

Leg buds

Fig. 1–4 Limb buds on the human embryo

The mechanism whereby the correct connections between tendons, muscles, and cartilage are established has still to be determined.[9]

This admission is very significant. If evolutionists do not know how a joint assembles itself, how can they be so sure that it evolved by a series of random genetic mistakes? The self-assembly of bones, ligaments and tendons represents a complicated and awesome task. Humans have never yet been able to design any machine that can build itself, let alone a machine containing many thousands of complex parts like the human body.

1.8 Critical nature of geometrical characteristics

The geometrical characteristics of a mechanism must generally be specified with much more precision than the material properties of the parts in the mechanism. This fact is well known in the field of mechanical engineering. For example, the geometrical characteristics in a mechanical watch, such as the shape of the gear teeth, must be specified within very close tolerances. If a geometrical characteristic, such as the shape of a gear tooth, is slightly in error, then the clock will cease to function. In contrast, if the material properties of the gear are changed slightly, then the watch will usually still be able to function. Often, the only impact of a new material is to change long-term aspects of performance such as how long the watch will last.

Despite the critical nature of geometrical characteristics, books on evolution virtually never mention them when discussing evolution. The evolution of new characteristics is generally described as a process where genes are gradually evolved and each new gene simply specifies more proteins. However, this description grossly underestimates what would actually be required for an organism to evolve because the cell must contain geometrical information about the organism. Whilst it is true that scientists do not yet understand how geometry is specified in an organism, this is not an excuse for ignoring the need for such information. There is no doubt that evolutionists avoid discussing geometrical information because such information presents a major problem for evolution.

The avoidance of critical characteristics can be seen in virtually every secular school and university biology textbook which discusses evolution. Biology textbooks often give examples of how a new colour of moth could plausibly evolve by gene mutation. The authors then argue that since colour could plausibly change in one step, it can be assumed that every single characteristic of the moth could change in single steps. But this argument makes the crucial mistake of assuming that all characteristics are as simple as colour. Even though the colour of a moth may be important to its survival, the characteristic of colour is nevertheless a trivial one in terms of how it affects the functioning of organs and parts within the moth. The supposed evolution of colour by gene mutation can never produce new mechanisms and therefore it does not demonstrate evolution. To prove the theory of evolution, the evolutionist would have to show how a geometrical characteristic, like the attachment position of a cruciate ligament, could evolve. However, this has never been done and can never be done because such a critical characteristic could not evolve in isolation.

The importance of geometrical characteristics can be illustrated with the analogy of car design. Just imagine going to a lecture on car design and hearing the speaker claim that the only thing needed to design a car is to specify the materials! Such a statement would be absolutely wrong because the car contains many mechanisms which need to be specified by many geometrical characteristics. In a similar way, it is very misleading for evolutionists to give the impression that an organism needs only to specify proteins in order to grow and function. The superficial nature of colour can also be illustrated with the analogy of car design. Just imagine someone arguing that since the colour of a car could change in one step, every characteristic of the car could evolve in single steps. This would be absolutely ridiculous because the geometrical characteristics of the car, such as the internal dimensions of the engine, are vastly more critical than the colour of the car. In a similar way, it is ridiculous to use colour change in organisms as an example of evolution.

1.9 Supreme design in the knee joint

The diagrams of the anatomy of the knee in Figs. 1–1 and 1–2 are deliberately simplified in order to identify the parts that are absolutely essential to the basic functioning of the knee. However, it is important to note that the complete knee has many other sophisticated parts that help to produce an efficient and strong joint. These parts include a bone at the front of the knee called the patella (knee-cap) and a fibrous capsule containing several ligaments which surrounds and supports the joint. There is also soft cartilage to reduce shock loads between the bones and an elaborate arrangement of muscle fibres connected to the front and back of the leg to enable the movement of the joint to be finely controlled. In addition, there is a lubricating fluid, called synovial fluid, inside the knee that makes the joint rotate smoothly and last a long time.

The biomechanics of the knee are also simplified in Fig. 1–2 for clarity. In reality the ligaments do stretch by a small amount when the knee is in certain positions. There is also a small amount of torsional freedom between the femur and tibia bones. These features make the knee joint an extremely sophisticated joint. Indeed, the knee joint is so sophisticated that human designers have been unable to produce an artificial knee that has anything approaching the performance of a real knee.

1.10 The human knee joint

The basic principle of the mammalian knee joint is unique whether it is the knee joint of an animal or human being. However, there is yet a further problem for evolution in that the human knee is distinctly different to the knees of monkeys and apes. In the case of humans, the knee is designed to lock conveniently in the standing position so that maintaining a vertical posture is easy. Also, the layout of the human knee enables humans to walk and run upright in a completely natural way. In the case of monkeys and apes, the knee cannot be straightened and must be continually loaded in flexion (bent leg). Evolutionists admit the fact that there is a big difference between the knee of animals and humans. For example, Dye says:

Despite the overall similarity of the design of the knee in tetrapods, no ideal animal model of the human knee is available.[10]

Evolutionists also admit that the only way apes can attempt to stand upright is by having awkward bends at the ankle, knee and hip joints.[11] Such a distorted posture means that apes can stay vertical for only short periods and distances. In contrast, an able-bodied and fit human being can walk and run many miles without great difficulty.

1.11 The limited effect of gene variation

When Charles Darwin first proposed his theory of evolution, he thought that the apparent changes in characteristics that normally appear in offspring could accumulate to produce new mechanisms. It is now known that these apparent changes in characteristics are produced by gene variation. It is also now known that gene variation has strict limits of change and cannot cause new mechanisms to appear as Darwin thought. This fact is now acknowledged by many evolutionists.

The reason why gene variation cannot produce new mechanisms is that gene variation involves only the shuffling of existing genes from the parents of the offspring. When two parents produce offspring, the offspring contain a unique mixture of genes from the parents. The only effect that gene variation can have is to change the expression of superficial characteristics such as size and colour. The limited change that can be produced by gene variation is demonstrated in selective breeding. For example, whilst it is possible to breed horses with extreme expressions of characteristics such as fast speed or great height, it is not possible to change a horse into another type of creature.

Gene variation has two very useful purposes. One purpose is to introduce beautiful variety into the world. This is particularly important in the case of the human being. Life would be very strange indeed if we all had an identical appearance! A second purpose of gene variation is that it enables a certain degree of adaptation to take place. For example, since moths sometimes have the genetic potential to produce a range of colours, they are able to adapt to changes in the colour of trees. If dark-coloured trees become more common than light-coloured trees in a particular area, it is an advantage for moths to have a darker colour since a darker colour is less conspicuous to predators such as birds. When it is an advantage to have a darker colour, it can be observed that the proportion of dark-coloured moths becomes greater than the proportion of light-coloured moths.

It should be noted that changes in colour and size represent very superficial changes and these cannot lead to the development of new mechanisms. It should also be noted that the ability of animals to adapt can be seen as an evidence of design because it is just what would be expected from a Creator who wanted creatures to fill the earth and survive changes in the environment.

1.12 The modern theory of evolution

According to the modern theory of evolution, the process by which organisms gain new characteristics is through genetic mistakes called 'gene mutations'. A gene mutation is typically the result of a copying error during reproduction and it produces a random change to the chemical information in the genetic code. Gene mutations in offspring are rare and only appear once in several thousand reproductions. Even though a gene mutation does change information in the genetic code, it cannot be assumed that the change could ever lead to the evolution of a new mechanism.

Current evidence shows that, in the vast majority of cases, gene mutations are very harmful. For example, gene mutations are known to be responsible for serious genetic disorders such as haemophilia and cystic fibrosis.[12] Even in cases where gene mutations do not cause serious harm, they certainly do not create any new mechanisms. No gene mutation has ever been identified that has produced a new mechanism or increased information in the genetic code.[13] Despite the absence of any evidence of mutations that have produced a new mechanism, evolutionists believe that over millions of years, millions of genetic mistakes have produced all the complex mechanisms that exist in nature.

Some evolutionists have recently claimed that evolution occurs in a punctuated equilibrium where there are periods of stability followed by relatively rapid change. It is important to realise however that punctuated equilibrium does not change the fact that evolution relies on an accumulation of small changes to characteristics. Punctuated equilibrium simply postulates that there are relatively long periods when there are few selective pressures and then relatively short periods of intense selective pressures.

It is important to recognise that the modern-day theory of evolution proposes that evolution does not occur in the vast majority of a population of organisms. The modern-day theory of evolution proposes that evolution happens only when reproduction goes wrong through gene mutation. Also, when a person has a deformity or disease due to a gene mutation, according to evolution this must be seen as a very necessary part of life because it is nature's way of experimenting with the design of a human being. According to evolution, without such experimentation and suffering, humans would never have evolved from primitive creatures.

Evolutionists fully acknowledge the cruel nature of the theory of evolution. One evolutionist has said the following:

The essential feature of Darwinian evolution is its accidental nature. Mutations occur by blind chance, and as a result of these purely random alterations in the characteristics of the organisms nature is provided with a wide range of options with which to select on the basis of suitability and advantage. In this way, complex organised structures can arise from the accumulation of vast numbers of small accidents. The corresponding increase in order (fall in entropy) occasioned by this trend is more than paid for by the much greater number of damaging mutations which are weeded out by natural selection. There is thus no conflict with the second law of thermodynamics. Today's beautifully fashioned creatures sit atop a family tree festooned with genetic disasters.[14]

Notice in this quote that the author admits that evolution works by an 'accumulation of vast numbers of small accidents'. Also notice how the author admits that a great number of genetic disasters are an essential part of the process of evolution.

The damaging nature of gene mutations shows the foolishness of believing that God could use evolution to create the world (theistic evolution). Gene mutations cause enormous suffering and it is inconceivable that an infinitely wise and loving Creator could ever choose to use such a process. It is also important to point out that an irreducible mechanism cannot evolve by gene mutation even if an intelligent being is able to select which gene should mutate in each step.

1.13 The deception of evolutionary theory

Evolutionists cannot give a single example of how one type of creature has evolved into another type of creature. The complete absence of examples of evolution means that evolutionists must employ strategies for explaining how evolution could supposedly work. As we have already seen, one tactic is to focus on superficial characteristics. Two other deceptive strategies that are commonly used are to focus on peripheral parts or to focus on a gradual increase in size.

FOCUS ON PERIPHERAL PARTS

A peripheral part is a part which is not essential to the functioning of a mechanism. For example, the glass front on a mechanical watch provides a useful cover but it is not essential for the watch to function. It is always possible to argue that a peripheral part could evolve by chance. However, even if peripheral parts could evolve, this does not mean that essential parts could evolve. When discussing the theory of evolution, evolutionists will deliberately discuss only peripheral parts of a mechanism without explaining this to the reader or audience. They will then argue that since some parts could have evolved by chance, all the parts of the mechanism could have evolved by chance. Any reader who does not realise that only peripheral parts have been mentioned may then be convinced that evolution can really work.

A common example of where evolutionists focus on peripheral parts is the eye. Evolutionists argue that the lens is not essential for the functioning of the eye and so one can imagine an eye without a lens evolving into an eye with a lens. They then try to convince the reader that every single part of the eye could have evolved step by step. However, this reasoning is false because there is an irreducible mechanism in the eye. Each individual light-sensitive cell consists of several parts such as photosensitive regions and a region for making connections with the optic nerve fibre. The optic nerve fibre, which transmits signals from the retina to the brain, also consists of several parts such as the connecting region and signal path. There is also an essential need for processing parts in the brain to make vision possible. Therefore, it is impossible for a light-sensitive eye cell to evolve since such cells have no functional use except as part of a fully functioning eye.

A similar situation exists for the knee joint. When evolutionists attempt to discuss the evolution of the knee, they describe how the knee-cap is not actually essential and how it just appeared and was retained because it gave advantages. They also say that the lubricating fluid was not essential but that it suddenly appeared and remained because it gave advantages. After giving several such examples, they try to convince the reader that every single part of the knee could just evolve by chance. But this argument is false because there is an irreducible mechanism at the core of the knee joint.

FOCUS ON SIZE

Evolutionists often focus on how an organ could theoretically evolve from a small organ into a larger organ. For example, Richard Dawkins argues that one can imagine a 'simple' eye with only a few light cells gradually evolving into a 'complex' eye which has thousands of cells.[15] However, this argument is flawed because an eye which has a few light-sensitive cells has components which are just as complex as an eye with thousands of cells. The main complexity in the eye lies within the design of each individual light-sensitive cell and not in the number of cells.

1.14 The deception of evolving words

Another strategy used by evolutionists to attempt to give evidence for evolution is to argue that the evolution of living creatures is analogous to the evolution of sentences of words. Words are used to represent information in the genetic code and their change is used to show how information in the genetic code could supposedly evolve over time. For example, Richard Dawkins uses the following sequence of words to model the supposed process of evolution:[16]

LFHGUXSBX	(jumble of letters)
MFHGUXSBX	(first beneficial mutation – characteristic labelled 'M')
MFHGUISBX	(second beneficial mutation – characteristic labelled 'I')
MF GUISBX	(third beneficial mutation – characteristic labelled ' ')
MF TUISBX	(fourth beneficial mutation – characteristic labelled 'T')
MF THISBX	(fifth beneficial mutation – characteristic labelled 'H')
MF THISBS	(sixth beneficial mutation – characteristic labelled 'S')
MF THISKS	(seventh beneficial mutation – characteristic labelled 'K')
ME THISKS	(eighth beneficial mutation – characteristic labelled 'E')
ME THINKS	(ninth beneficial mutation – characteristic labelled 'N')

Each new set of letters is supposed to represent a slightly changed organism with one single new improved characteristic. After accumulating many changes, the final sentence is supposed to represent the genetic code of a new type of organism with a new mechanism. It is important to notice here that evolutionists admit that evolution only works by changing one characteristic at a time.

At first sight, the evolution of words might seem convincing. However, the use of letters enables the evolutionist to obscure the fact that real organisms have interdependencies and critical characteristics. To illustrate why words cannot demonstrate evolution, let us assume that each of the letters in the words *ME THINKS* represents one of the critical characteristics of the knee joint as follows (refer to Fig. 1–3):

M	= Position of ligament attachment point 1 (Femur)
E	= Position of ligament attachment point 2 (Femur)
T	= Position of ligament attachment point 3 (Tibia)
H	= Position of ligament attachment point 4 (Tibia)
I	= Assembly of anterior cruciate ligament to point 1
N	= Assembly of anterior cruciate ligament to point 4
K	= Assembly of posterior cruciate ligament to point 2
S	= Assembly of posterior cruciate ligament to point 3

It is now clear that all of these characteristics are actually *interdependent* and *critical* and must exist simultaneously! In his evolutionary sequence, Dawkins assumes that when the first correct letter (in this case M) is selected, it will improve the system. However, in the case of the four-bar hinge, getting one single characteristic such as the position of one attachment point correct whilst all of the other characteristics are incorrect would result in a useless, non-functioning system! Therefore, only when the letters read *ME THINKS* is it possible for the four-bar hinge to function.

1.15 The deception of evolving pictures

Another abstract model of evolution which is used by Richard Dawkins involves the evolution of pictures from simple lines to complex images.[17] Starting with just one line, Dawkins applies a variety of rules for branching off lines and evolving patterns in an incremental way. Some of the rules inevitably produce interesting patterns that give a pictorial resemblance of such things as bats and insects, and so there is a claim that this demonstrates evolution. However, just because it is possible to evolve a picture does not mean that it is possible to evolve a living organism. A picture does not have any interacting parts and therefore there is no requirement for the lines of the picture to exist simultaneously. If each line of the picture represented the different characteristics of a four-bar mechanism, then the picture could not evolve and its lines would have to appear simultaneously. As with letters and words, the use of a set of pictures to model an organism is completely invalid unless account is taken of the interdependent characteristics of the real physical system.

It is important not to confuse the complexity of a physical system with the apparent complexity of an inanimate object like a detailed picture. It does not matter how complicated a picture is, it does not perform physical functions with complex interactions. To claim that the evolution of a picture can demonstrate the evolution of a complex organism is absurd. Pictures are used to describe evolution because this enables the evolutionist to escape the real world of physically interacting systems.

The fact that evolutionists have to use jumbles of letters and pictures to explain evolution adds weight to the argument for design. If organisms could evolve, then the evolutionist would not have to make up abstract models in the first place. Nothing would be clearer or more convincing than to show how a real functioning mechanism such as the knee joint could have evolved.

1.16 The deception of Genetic Algorithms

Genetic algorithms (GAs) are modelling techniques which attempt to apply the theory of evolution to a real life problem such as the design of a new mechanism. The GA method of optimisation is now widely taught to undergraduate students in many disciplines including engineering and mathematics. Not surprisingly, there are claims that the use of GAs proves that evolution does work. However, when case studies are analysed, it is clear that GAs do not demonstrate evolution at all. In fact GAs provide a useful means of showing how evolution cannot work.

In order to apply a GA to the design of a new mechanism, an existing mechanism is described in terms of a set of characteristics. The existing mechanism is made to produce offspring (on paper!) with a new set of characteristics. The new characteristics are determined by gene variation or gene mutation. Offspring which are considered to be the fittest are selected for breeding the next generation of solutions. Offspring are continually evolved until no further improvements are needed or until no further improvements are possible. In practice it is found that GAs can produce optimal characteristics, such as size, in a mechanism. However, this is not surprising because gene variation is well able to produce beneficial changes to superficial characteristics, like size, in real organisms. When a GA breeds an optimised solution, there is no difference between this and the breeding of a thoroughbred horse.

The real test for GAs is whether or not they are able to produce new types of mechanisms. Despite years of research, this is something that GAs have not been able to do. For example, in one paper in the *Journal of Engineering Design,* a gene mutation is applied to the design code of a helicopter which results in the helicopter changing from a single rotor blade to a double rotor blade design.[18] Such a design change involves the changing of thousands of precise geometrical characteristics. Therefore, the researchers have to temporarily abandon the process of evolution and make the 'single' mutation represent thousands of simultaneous changes. Such intervention means that the researchers were actually modelling an 'intelligent' design process and not an evolutionary process at all! The use of GAs in this instance actually showed that evolution of physical systems cannot take place.

Research into engineering design practice in industry has actually shown that the best method of design is to be as concurrent as possible[19,20] which essentially means to bring information together simultaneously. This conclusion shows that the best way of designing is to be as different as possible to the process of evolution!

1.17 Lessons from engineering design

The supposed process of evolution is the complete opposite to the process of design used by human designers. Evolution is a 'bottom-up' process that supposedly starts with details and finishes with a concept. In contrast, human designers design in a 'top-down' process starting with concepts and finishing with details. Engineers throughout the world are taught that the engineering design process must be a top-down process which starts with fully functioning concepts.[21,22,23] The reason why designers are taught to design in a top-down way is that engineering contains many irreducible mechanisms and these mechanisms cannot be designed from the bottom up. Since engineering and nature contain similar mechanisms and since human designers have found that they must design from the top down, this provides yet further evidence against evolution.

The top-down process of engineering design is demonstrated in the design of bridges. When designing a bridge, a designer first of all chooses between different concepts such as a suspension bridge, truss bridge and cable stay bridge. After selecting the concept, the designer then designs all the details such as the connections and beams. It would be ridiculous for a designer to begin the design of a bridge by evolving a simple plate of material and hoping that it would eventually turn into a bridge. Such an approach would get nowhere because a single crude piece of material cannot turn into complex layouts in single steps.

It is interesting to note that four-bar mechanisms are commonly used in mechanical engineering. For example, four-bar mechanisms are often used in the steering systems of four-wheel drive motor vehicles. The theory of evolution is analogous to proposing that one can take the engineering drawings of a simple pivot joint used in a motorbike steering wheel and evolve them into the drawings of the steering system of a four-wheeled vehicle. The information on the drawings is equivalent to the genetic code, and random photocopying errors in the information are analogous to gene mutations. The evolutionist believes that the random photocopying errors will sometimes produce a slightly better system and that eventually the steering system will turn into a four-bar mechanism and form the steering system of a four-wheeled vehicle!

Such reasoning is absurd for several reasons. Firstly, if a random change is made to the information on a drawing of a motorbike steering system, this will at best cause no change in the basic functions and at worst have fatal consequences. Secondly, there are no intermediate mechanisms between a motorbike steering system and a car steering system whereas evolution would require hundreds of fully functioning intermediate forms. In a similar way, it is impossible for the knee joint to have evolved from a simple pivot joint by copying errors in the genetic code.

1.18 The effect of the Fall

Whilst the knee joint contains supreme design, it is also subject to diseases such as arthritis. Genesis 3 teaches that God put a curse on the whole of creation as a judgement for the sin and rebellion of Adam and Eve. In the case of human beings, the judgement involved undesirable effects such as aging, illness and mortality. Even though there are signs of the curse on creation, it is still possible to see clear evidence of design. It is important to point out that gene mutations are part of the curse on mankind and only existed after the rebellion of Adam and Eve. It is ironic that evolutionists consider gene mutations as the creator of life, when in fact gene mutations are a part of the curse which has brought death into the world. It is also sad that many theologians believe that God used evolution to create the world.

1.19 The power and wisdom of God in creation

The irreducibility of the mammalian knee joint provides powerful evidence that the natural world has a Designer. However, the extreme elegance, efficiency and durability of the knee joint also gives evidence of the infinite power and wisdom of that Designer. The knee joint is just one example of design in nature that shows the truth of the biblical statement that 'His [God's] invisible attributes are clearly seen, being understood by the things that are made' (Romans 1:20). In the Old Testament, Solomon spoke of the wonder of the growth of bones in the womb: 'As you do not know what is the way of the wind, or how the bones grow in the womb of her who is with child, so you do not know the works of God who makes everything' (Ecclesiastes 11:5). Recent studies of the growth of joints have shown the remarkable truth of these verses.

Notes on Chapter 1

1   A paper on the knee joint, based on the contents of this chapter, has been published in the *AIG Technical Journal* entitled: 'Critical characteristics and the irreducible knee joint', *CET Journal,* Vol. 13, No.2, 1999. This paper has also been translated into German and published in the German Journal Factum: 'Das Design des Kniegelenks', *Factum,* No. 6, pp 14–18, 2000.

2   **Darwin, C.,** (1872), *Origin of species,* 6th Ed., New York University Press, New York, p. 154, 1988.

3   **Dawkins, R.,** *The blind watchmaker*, Penguin, p. 91, 1986.

4   **Behe, M.J.,** *Darwin's black box*, Free Press, 1996.

5   **Segal, P.** and **Jacob, M.,** *The knee*, Wolfe, p. 9, 1983.

6   **O'Connor, J.** and **Goodfellow, J.,** 'The mechanics of the knee and prosthesis design', *Journal of bone and joint surgery,* 60B, pp. 358–369, 1978.

7   **Guyot, J.,** *Atlas of Human Limb Joints*, Springer-Verlag, p. 20, 1981.

8   **Gould, S.J.,** 'Is a new and general theory of evolution emerging?' *Paleobiology,* Vol. 6(1), p.127, January 1980.

9   **Wolpert, L., (ed.)** *Principles of development*, Oxford University Press, p. 316, 1998.

10   **Scott, F. and Dye, M.D.,** 'An evolutionary perspective of the knee', *Journal of bone and joint surgery* (1987) 69A, pp. 976–983, 1987.

11   **Hinchliffe, J.R. and Johnson, D.R.,** *The development of the vertebrate limb,* Clarendon Press, pp. 37–39, 1980.

12   **Roberts, M.B.V.,** *Biology a functional approach*, 4th Ed, Nelson, p. 593, 1986.

13   **Spetner, L.** *Not by chance*, The Judaica Press, Brooklyn, New York, 1997.

14   **Davies, P.,** *God and the new physics*, Penguin, p. 166, 1983.

15   **Dawkins, R.,** *op. cit.,* p. 81.

16   **Dawkins, R.,** *op. cit.,* p. 48.

17   **Dawkins, R.,** *op. cit.,* p. 52.

18   **Crossley, W.A. and Laananen, D.H.,** 'The Genetic Algorithm as an automated methodology for helicopter conceptual design', *Journal of engineering design,* Vol. 8, No. 3, 1997.

19   **Sohlenius, G.,** 'Concurrent Engineering', *Annals of the CIRP,* Vol. 41, No. 2, pp. 645–655, 1992.

20   **Salzberg, S. and Watkins, M.,** 'Managing information for concurrent engineering: challenges and barriers', *Research in Engineering Design,* No. 2, pp. 35–52, 1990.

21   **Pahl, G.** and **Beitz, W.,** *Engineering Design—A systematic Approach*, 2nd Edition, Springer, pp. 61–69, 1996.

22   **Shigley, J.E.,** *Mechanical Engineering Design*, 3rd Edition, McGraw Hill, pp. 4–6, 1977.

23   **British Standard BS 7000.** *Guide to managing product design*, p. 17, 1989.

The irreducible flight mechanisms of birds

Then God said, 'Let the waters abound with an abundance of living creatures, and let birds fly above the earth across the face of the firmament of the heavens.' So God created great sea creatures and every living thing that moves, with which the waters abounded, according to their kind, and every winged bird according to its kind. And God saw that it was good (Genesis 1:20–21).

The Bible teaches that birds were created as fully formed flying creatures and that birds have not evolved from land creature as claimed in the theory of evolution. In fact, the Bible teaches that birds were created before land creatures. Modern discoveries about the very demanding requirements of flight have provided overwhelming evidence that birds must have been created as fully formed flying creatures. This chapter describes some of the intricate and irreducible mechanisms which are required for bird flight. It also shows how the irreducibility of flight is demonstrated by the history of aviation.

2.1 Irreducible mechanisms for gliding

Fig. 2–1 shows some of the essential mechanisms required for gliding. Even though gliding may appear to be a simple form of flight, it is not simple at all. Gliding requires the simultaneous existence of several precise mechanisms including aerofoil wings, light structures and control mechanisms.

I AEROFOIL WINGS
The aerofoil cross-section of a bird wing is shown in Fig. 2–2. The leading

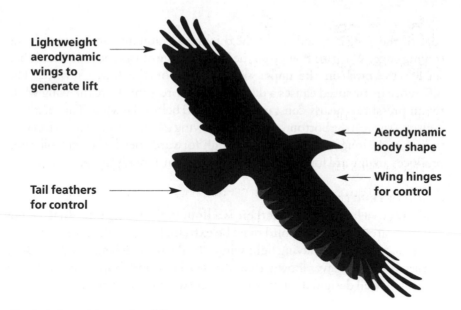

Lightweight aerodynamic wings to generate lift

Aerodynamic body shape

Wing hinges for control

Tail feathers for control

Fig. 2–1 Essential parts for gliding

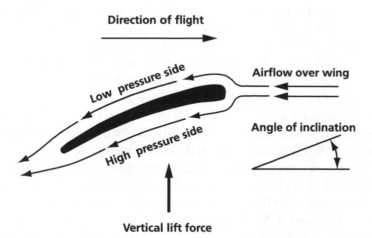

Direction of flight

Low pressure side

Airflow over wing

High pressure side

Angle of inclination

Vertical lift force

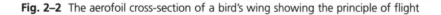

Fig. 2–2 The aerofoil cross-section of a bird's wing showing the principle of flight

edge of the wing is rounded and the thickness gradually tapers towards the trailing edge. When air flows past the leading edge of the aerofoil, the air has further to travel on the upper surface than on the lower surface. The difference in air speed causes a decrease in air pressure above the wing while the air pressure is nearly constant or increased below the wing. The relatively high pressure on the bottom surface of the wing produces an upward force on the wing. As long as the bird has enough forward speed, the aerofoil wing produces an upward force which keeps the bird in a steady glide.

II LIGHT STRUCTURES

Air has such a low density that there is a limit to the lifting force that a wing can generate. Therefore, a bird must be extremely light to enable gliding to take place. As well as having light wings, birds must also have light bodies. Modern studies have shown that the feathers and bones of birds are supremely well designed for producing lightweight structures.

III CONTROL MECHANISMS

Other essential mechanisms for gliding are control mechanisms. A bird must be able to have fine control of wing and tail movement in order to achieve stable and safe gliding. In particular, a bird must have mechanisms to change altitude, direction and speed. To change altitude, the lift force on the wings must be controlled by applying fine adjustments to the angle of inclination of the wings. If the angle of inclination of the wings is not controlled finely enough, the bird could experience unstable flight and drop from the sky. To change the direction of flight requires banking to the left or right. This can be achieved by inclining the wings at different angles in order to produce a different lift force on the two wings and thus tilt the bird into a turn. Banking is a particularly difficult manoeuvre because it also causes a different drag force on the two wings. This inequality of drag forces would put the bird into an unstable spin if there were no other compensating forces being generated. A bird generates such compensating forces by moving other flight feathers such as the tail feathers.

One of the most difficult challenges of flight is that of slowing down sharply before landing. To slow down, a bird spreads out its wings and tail feathers in order to greatly increase the amount of drag on the bird. This manoeuvre requires split-second timing and precise control in order to be carried out safely. Some birds even have a special group of feathers on the leading edge of their wings called the 'alula' to help give the bird stability at low speeds. The alula contains three to six small stiff feathers and these form a small slot at the leading edge of the wing at low flight speeds. This slot has the effect of squeezing and speeding up airflow across the top of the wing, thus reducing the effects of slow-speed turbulence and thus helping to prevent an unstable stall. It is interesting to note that modern aircraft have a similar feature to the alula for the same aerodynamic reasons. The slot in aircraft is sometimes called the 'Handley Page slot'.

There are thousands of species of flying bird and they all have the essential mechanisms of aerofoil wings, lightweight structures and control mechanisms. These mechanisms are not found in land animals and indeed they would be a hindrance to them. There are such vast differences between the requirements of gliding and land locomotion that birds could not have evolved from land animals and must have been designed to be fully functioning as birds from the beginning of their existence.

2.2 Irreducible mechanisms for powered flight

The fact that a bird requires several sophisticated sub-systems for gliding alone shows that it cannot be the product of evolution. However, virtually all birds can also perform powered flight for long distances. Powered flight requires all the sub-systems of gliding plus additional parts such as a special breastbone and large wing muscles. The breastbone in a bird is unique because it has a long extension for attaching the wing muscles. This long extension is called a keel.

Evolutionists fully admit that birds need many specialised sub-systems simultaneously in place for flying. However, they cannot explain how these sub-systems could have evolved in small steps by genetic mistakes. One advanced book on the structure of birds says this about the requirements of flight:

The anatomical requirements of flight include not only these limitations on total body weight, but also a general streamlining of the body, virtually total commitment of the forelimb to flight, a specialised pectoral girdle and wing bones, modification of the thoracic musculature for flight, and accentuation of the special sense organs, especially vision and balance, with corresponding enlargement and modification of the brain. Finally the energetics of flight impose special demands on the respiratory and circulatory systems.[1]

2.3 Irreducible feathers

A flight feather is a masterpiece of design and is one of the most efficient structures known to man. A flight feather is shown in Fig. 2–3. It consists of a hierarchy of structures. The main feather stem comes first, then the barbs and finally the barbules. The main stem consists of a hollow structure that contains air or foam to give it an extremely high stiffness to weight ratio. The stem starts off as a circle near the root of the feather. The cross-section of the stem then changes into a rectangular shape which is more structurally efficient.

The stem has a massed array of barbs on each side that form the basic feather shape. Each barb itself has two sets of barbules. The barbules on

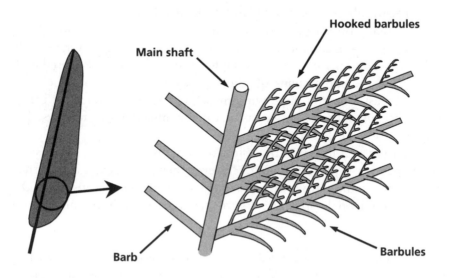

Fig. 2–3 Flight feather

one side have a set of hooks whilst the barbules on the other side are plain. Therefore, the hooked barbules can interlock with the plain barbules on the adjacent barb. The hooks and barbules are arranged so that they prevent air going through them when the wing is pushed downwards but they allow air to pass through them when the wing is being pulled upwards.[2] This feature enables the bird to maximise the efficiency of flapping by only allowing the wing to push down on the air. The hooked structure of the feather gives it a lightweight flat surface which is ideal for producing an aerodynamic flapping force. A large bird can have up to hundreds of thousands of barbules in a single flight feather and these combine to give a very high level of stiffness and strength.

According to evolution, the feather evolved by a long series of genetic mistakes. However, feathers are irreducible structures which require many parts to be simultaneously present for the feather to be of any use. The interlocking mechanism of the barbules alone shows an amazing level of interdependency because the barbs and barbules must all be in place simultaneously for the feather to function. Feathers are also unique to birds. There is not a single known land creature that has any structures or mechanisms resembling a feather. The irreducibility and uniqueness of feathers gives great evidence of design.

The hierarchical structure of the feather also presents a big problem for evolution. Structural hierarchies are often used in engineering structures such as bridges and buildings. A structural hierarchy requires great planning and creativity to achieve because the parts are so interdependent. Engineers know that a structural hierarchy can never be produced by a process of incremental change. In a similar way, the hierarchical structure of the feather provides powerful evidence of design.

Evolutionists admit that the feather is an amazing structure. For example, Jack Cohen, who carried out extensive research into bird feathers, has said the following:

The feather is the sum of the debris of some 1.5×10^7 [15 million] to 5×10^9 [5 billion] cells exactly organised and engineered to the utmost precision...Some idea of the complexity of a feather should first be acquired by simple examination. Too few biologists have looked closely at this structure; it is a humbling process.[3]

Notice in this quotation the term 'engineered to the utmost precision'. This is the kind of terminology that many evolutionists try not to use because it sounds as though the feather has been designed. The fact that evolutionists are sometimes forced to use the language of design demonstrates that there is design in nature. It is also interesting how Cohen describes the study of a feather as a 'humbling process'. It is amazing how so many modern biologists can marvel at the complexity of the feather and yet deny that the feather has a Creator.

2.4 Irreducible wing bones

Most birds have wing bones which are a hollow tubular shape. Such a shape is very efficient for providing strength and stiffness. However, some larger birds like vultures have an additional structure inside their bones to make the bones even more structurally efficient. The additional structure inside the bone is a type of truss structure,[4] as shown in Fig. 2–4. According to the theory of evolution, the truss bone has evolved from a hollow tubular bone by an accumulation of genetic mistakes. However, engineers know that it is impossible to evolve such a truss structure from a hollow tubular bone because the design characteristics (or variables) of a truss structure are fundamentally different to those of a solid beam.

If an attempt is made to incrementally improve the structural efficiency of a prismatic beam (beam with uniform cross section), then it always becomes another type of prismatic beam. For example, a solid circular beam could conceivably turn into a hollow circular beam but it cannot turn into a non-prismatic structure. Researchers have found that to produce a truss structure with cross bracing, like the one shown in Fig. 2–4, by a

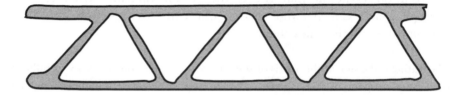

Fig. 2–4 Truss structure inside a wing bone of a large bird

process of incremental change, it is necessary to have some sort of bracing right from the start.[5] In general, different structural forms, like truss structures and beams, are so distinct that they cannot be optimised from each other. For example, R. W. Birmingham has said:

In structural design the choice of structural type, often termed 'form', is crucial. Caldwell demonstrated that with some structures no amount of optimisation of a specific structural form can regain the loss of performance due to selecting a non-optimal form at the outset...The alternative structural forms can be of such different natures that it is not a matter of changing the values of the variables involved, but of changing the variables themselves.[6,7]

2.5 Irreducible mechanisms for migration

The main purpose of migration is to enable birds to move to warmer countries in the winter. Even though birds are small, they have incredible sensors within their bodies, some of which are still a mystery to scientists. Birds are believed to use many cues for navigation including the sun, stars, time, polarised light, ultraviolet light, smell, infrasound, the magnetic field, gravity and pressure.[8] Migration is irreducible because it requires several mechanisms to exist simultaneously. For example, it is no use only being able to use the sun and stars to navigate because when the weather is overcast, there would be nothing to follow.

Any advanced book on birds will acknowledge that navigation in birds is so complicated and sophisticated that modern science is unable to explain it, let alone replicate it or describe how it could have evolved. One advanced book on birds says:

As yet, not enough is known to reveal any complex or complexes of orientational and navigational systems which can fully account for what the birds themselves do actually achieve.[9]

This admission raises the question: If scientists do not fully understand how birds navigate, then how can they be sure that navigation evolved by genetic mistakes? Birds perform some of the most astounding feats imaginable in navigation. Three of the most spectacular examples include migration by the Arctic tern, the bar-headed goose and the golden plover. A summary of the migration of these birds is as follows:

I ARCTIC TERN

One of the longest migratory paths possible is that of a return journey between the North and South Pole. This route also involves the greatest changes in temperature! Despite the extreme nature of this route, it is the exact migratory path followed by the Arctic tern. Arctic terns spend the northern summer in the Arctic, where they rear their young. After the short northern summer, they fly south over 15,000 km to the Antarctic to stay in the southern summer. One remarkable aspect of this journey is the sheer distance. Even though the bird weighs just a few tens of grams, it is able to travel these vast distances every year. Since terns sometimes live for 30 years or more, they may travel nearly a million kilometres in their lifetime. Another remarkable aspect of the journey is the complexity of the navigational requirement. If the Arctic tern uses the stars to navigate, then it must recognise stars in both hemispheres. If the bird uses the earth's magnetic field, then it must know the difference between the south magnetic pole and the north magnetic pole!

II BAR-HEADED GOOSE

One of the highest possible migratory routes is a route over the Himalayas, which contain the highest mountains in the world. Despite the great altitude of the Himalayas, the bar-headed goose travels across this mountain range during its migration. One remarkable aspect of this journey is that the goose must start from sea level and then gain 9 km in altitude.[10] A second remarkable aspect is that at an altitude of 9 km there is very little oxygen. At this altitude most creatures, including humans, would not survive the lack of oxygen. Not only can the bar-headed goose survive the altitude, but it can also consistently fly great distances at this altitude.

III GOLDEN PLOVER

One of the most precarious migratory routes is a journey from Alaska to Hawaii. This journey is about 3000 km in length and the island of

Hawaii represents a tiny target in the vast expanse of the Pacific Ocean. Yet, the golden plover undertakes this journey without training!

2.6 The irreducibility of man-made flying machines

The impossibility of the evolution of flight is clearly demonstrated by the history of aviation. Some of the main historical milestones of technology and aviation are shown in Table 2–1.[11] The table shows that the first controlled flying machine was produced in 1902, over 150 years after the beginning of the development of sophisticated machinery. This huge period of time was not due to any lack of desire to make a flying machine but was due to the great difficulty engineers had in working out how to design a machine that could fly in a controlled manner.

Table 2–1 Development of man-made flying machines

EVENT	DATE
▶ Development of sophisticated machinery	1750–1800
▶ Invention of aerofoil	1804
▶ Development of ultra-light wing structures	1896
▶ Invention of tail wing	1896
▶ Invention of tail fin	1902
▶ Invention of tail rudder	1902
▶ First controlled gliding	1902
▶ First controlled powered aeroplane	1903
▶ First controlled powered helicopter	1907

Even though many sophisticated machines and engines were developed in the industrial revolution between 1750 and 1800, there was very little progress in the development of man-made flying machines during this time. When the aerofoil wing was discovered in 1804, some people thought that it would not take long at all to produce a flying machine because wings are the most obvious parts that are necessary for flight. However, despite the design of aerofoil wings in 1804, there was still a huge gap of 98 years before the first controlled glide was achieved in 1902. The length of time it took to develop flight is remarkable considering how many talented scientists and engineers worked on the challenge and that they were supported by the study of flight in birds.

The reason why it took so long to develop the first controlled flying machine after the discovery of the aerofoil is that flight requires lightweight structures and flight control mechanisms as well as aerofoil wings. In addition, these mechanisms generally do not exist in non-flying machines and so engineers had to develop the mechanisms from scratch. Even though there were sophisticated machines in the nineteenth century such as steam engines and pumps, these were useless for the purposes of flight.

During the nineteenth century, engineers had to use great creativity and foresight to design novel lightweight structures that were suitable for flight. Engineers also demonstrated great intellectual skill in understanding the mechanics of flight and designing the necessary control mechanisms for a flying machine. Control of flight is very difficult because a flying machine is completely unrestrained in the air and there must be controls for producing the right orientation of the aircraft in all three axes of pitch, roll and yaw. In the case of a car, it is only necessary to control the direction of the car on the road (the yaw angle). However, in the case of an aircraft, it can roll from side to side and it can pitch up and down. An additional challenge with flight is that it is necessary to fly within certain limits of speed and orientation in order to maintain stability.

In 1902 the Wright brothers made some famous inventions which enabled the successful development of the first properly controlled glider. Previous developers had designed light wing structures and produced elevation control by hinged panels. However, no one had properly understood the problems of banking due to the different drag forces on the two wings. When the Wright brothers studied this problem they set about designing a device to counteract this difference in drag. The device which they invented was the tail-fin rudder and this was found to be a very good solution for producing a stabilising force during a turn. The tail-fin rudder is analogous to the tail feathers of a bird and it is likely that the Wright brothers realised that birds use their tail feathers for control. The invention of the tail-fin rudder enabled the Wright brothers to carry out the first successful glide in 1902.

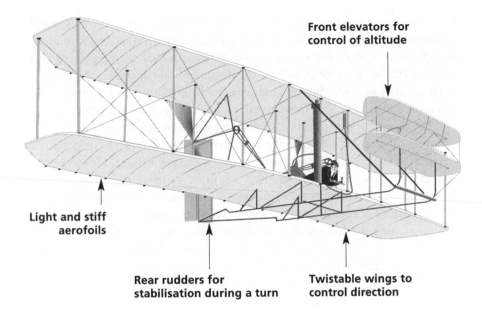

Front elevators for control of altitude

Light and stiff aerofoils

Rear rudders for stabilisation during a turn

Twistable wings to control direction

Fig. 2–5 The Wright Flyer

In 1903 the Wright brothers went further when they produced the first controlled powered aircraft called *The Flyer*, which is shown in Fig. 2–5. Notice that the first controlled glide took 98 years to produce following the discovery of the aerofoil, whereas the first powered flight came only one year after the first controlled glide. This clearly demonstrates that gliding is not a simple form of flight compared to powered flight as some biology books claim.

The delicate nature of flight is demonstrated by the number of accidents that occurred during flight trials in the nineteenth century. A history book on aviation gives this account of a brave Frenchman who had a narrow escape:

In 1857 Jean-Marie Le Bris built an elegant glider whose shape was based on the albatrosses he had seen... After the glider had again been launched downhill it once more carried Le Bris for a short distance through the air, but as he had no means of control he was unable to avoid a crash-landing in which he broke his leg.[12]

This example illustrates the kind of problem that land animals would experience if they attempted to experiment with flight. Experimenting with flight is a good way of becoming extinct, not of turning into a bird! Notice in the above quotation how the designer had tried to copy the design of the albatross. Even though engineers had the example of flying birds, it still took man a long time to work out how to design flying machines.

If the theory of evolution were true and it was possible to evolve flight by incremental steps, it should have been possible for engineers to get a land vehicle like a steam train and evolve it step by step for flight. However, such a proposal is absurd because there is a fantastic difference between a land vehicle and an aircraft. In the same way, it is absurd to propose that a land-based creature gradually evolved into a flying creature.

Considering the complexities of flight, it is really no surprise that it took over a century and a half to develop the first controlled flying machine after the development of the first machines in the industrial revolution. Such a long development demonstrates that flight cannot evolve by random accidents.

2.7 Modern aeronautical engineering

The difficulty of designing flight mechanisms is demonstrated by the fact that it takes three or four years to gain a degree qualification in aerospace engineering. Such hard study would not be necessary if flight could simply be evolved step by step.

The method that engineers employ to design an aeroplane also shows why a process of evolution cannot produce flight. Like all other engineers, aerospace engineers always design from the top down starting with a complete concept and then finalising the details at the end.[13] The first step in the design process is to specify the required principal functions such as the size of the aircraft, its maximum speed and its range. Having clarified the high level functions, an overall concept is designed which defines major details like the layout of wings and the number of power units. Having designed the overall concept, much system analysis is carried out to make sure that the sub-systems combine to produce the overall desired effect. Finally, the detailed design of each part in the plane is finalised and all the parts will be present and fully functioning from the first production model.

Imagine how absurd it would be to attempt to design a plane in an evolutionary bottom-up process. Evolution would supposedly start with an insignificant detail like a single rivet or bar of metal. Such a crude part would then supposedly evolve with other parts and these would assemble themselves and eventually become an integrated aeroplane! Such a process is of course ridiculous because parts like wings have no use except as part of a fully functioning aircraft.

2.8 The fossil record of birds

Birds are so different from other creatures that there would have been hundreds of thousands of intermediate forms between birds and land animals if birds had evolved. With such a large number of intermediate forms, it is certain that they would be evident in the fossil record. However, what has actually been found is a complete absence of intermediate forms in the fossil record, as shown by Gish.[14] One of the most unusual extinct birds is Archaeopteryx which is shown in Fig. 2–6. This bird is sometimes

Fig. 2–6 Archaeopteryx

quoted as an intermediate form, but modern studies have revealed that the fossil imprints show feathers that are identical to those of modern flying birds.[15] Since the feather is a complex structure and one of the most important components for flight, this makes Archaeopteryx no less advanced than any living bird. The fact that Archaeopteryx had teeth and a bony tail is sometimes used as evidence that it was an intermediate form of animal. However, such features do not make it less of a bird. It was simply a bird that happened to have teeth and a bony tail. Some fish have teeth but this does not make them any less fish. The fact is that teeth and bony tails can have their uses on any type of creature.

Flight is supposed to have evolved independently in birds, mammals, reptiles and insects but there is a complete lack of intermediate forms of life between non-flying and flying in each case. The fact that these intermediate forms are missing means that the fossil record completely supports the concept of the instantaneous creation of flying creatures.

2.9 Theories of evolved flight

Since there is no fossil evidence of the evolution of flight, and since only birds have feathers, it is very difficult for the evolutionist to attempt to explain how flight could have evolved. It is often speculated that birds evolved from reptiles. However, there are enormous conceptual differences between the two classes of creature such as structure, body temperature and metabolic rate. It is also suggested that the scales of reptiles frayed, gave survival advantages due to warmth and, from these frayed scales, flight feathers evolved. However, there is an enormous difference between scales and feathers and there is no evidence of any intermediate structures between scales and feathers. This is how one biology book describes the supposed evolution of flight in birds:

We believe that the wing must have evolved according to natural selection, an accumulation of favourable mutations each conferring a rather small selective advantage. If we follow this line of argument, the feather must have developed from a less efficient proto-feather, the wing from a less efficient proto-wing. A variant is the idea of a pre-adaptation: that the feather and the wing developed for some purpose other than flight, but proved well suited to flight at a later stage. This may sound far-fetched....[16]

Notice here how the author states that evolutionists 'believe' that the wing 'must have evolved' even though he knows of no evidence to support the theory. Such a statement shows how evolution is a theory that is believed through faith and not real evidence. Also notice how the author admits that the theory sounds 'far-fetched'.

It is ironic that whilst the evolution of flight is confidently taught as a fact to school children, advanced books on biology often make the admission that there is no evidence that birds evolved and not even a credible explanation of how they could have evolved. Professor Andy McIntosh, who is a senior academic in engineering science in the UK, has correctly summed up the importance of flight as evidence of design:

Flight alone demolishes any concept of evolution.[17]

A brief discussion of the irreducible flight mechanisms of birds and other flying creatures has been produced by Professor McIntosh.[18,19]

2.10 The power and wisdom of God in creation

The amazing design of birds reveals God's attributes of infinite power and wisdom. In the Old Testament book of Job, God reminds Job of his human limitations by posing a rhetorical question: 'Does the hawk fly by your wisdom...?' (Job 39:26). The wisdom required to design and make a living bird is completely beyond the capabilities of a human being. In fact, scientists cannot fully understand how birds function, let alone create a living bird. In the book of Proverbs, Agur speaks of the wonder of bird flight: 'There are three things which are too wonderful for me, yes, four which I do not understand: The way of an eagle in the air...' (Proverbs 30:18–19).

Notes on Chapter 2

1 **King, A.S. and McLelland, J.,** *Birds—their structure and form,* Bailliere Tindall, p. 5, 1984.

2 **King, A.S. and McLelland, J.,** *op. cit.,* p. 30.

3 **Cohen, J.,** 'Feathers and pattern', in *Advances in Morphogenesis* (Ed), Abercrombie, M. and Bracket, J, Academic Press, New York and London, p 9 & 12, 1966.

4   **Thompson, D.,** *On growth and form,* Cambridge University Press, p. 236, 1961.

5   **Nha Chu, D., Xie, Y. M., Hira, A. and Steven, G.P.,** 'Evolutionary structural optimisation for problems with stiffness constraints', *Finite elements in analysis and design,* Vol 21, pp. 239–251, 1996.

6   **Birmingham, R.W.,** *A graphical exploration of the interaction of material and form in structural design,* PhD Thesis, Newcastle University, pp. 25–29, 1994.

7   **Caldwell, J.B. and Woodhead, R.G.,** 'Ship structures: some possibilities for improvement', *Transactions of the North East Coast Institute of Engineers and Shipbuilders,* Vol 89, p. 101–120, 1973.

8   **King, A.S. and McLelland, J.,** *op. cit.,* pp. 279–283.

9   **King, A.S. and McLelland, J.,** *op. cit.,* p. 282.

10   **King, A.S. and McLelland, J.,** *op. cit.,* pp. 5–6.

11   **Baldry, D.** (Editor), *The Hamlyn history of aviation,* Hamlyn, 1996.

12   **Baldry, D.** (Editor), *op. cit.,* p. 14.

13   **Raymer, D.P.,** *Aircraft Design,* AIAA, 1992.

14   **Gish, D.,** *Evolution: the challenge of the fossil record,* Creation Life Publishers, p. 110, 1985.

15   **King, A.S. and McLelland, J.,** *op. cit.,* p. 1.

16   **Hinchliffe, J.R. and Johnson, D.R.,** *The development of the vertebrate limb,* Clarendon Press, p. 49, 1980.

17   **McIntosh, A.C.,** *Genesis for today,* Day One, p. 172, 1997.

18   **McIntosh, A.C.,** *Flight,* pamphlet 322, Creation Science Movement, Portsmouth, 1999.

19   **Ashton, J. (Editor),** *In six days—why 50 scientists choose to believe in creation,* New Holland, pp. 146–154, 1999.

The irreducible earth ecosystem

For thus says the Lord, who created the heavens, who is God, who formed the earth and made it, who has established it, who did not create it in vain, who formed it to be inhabited (Isaiah 45:18).

The Bible teaches that the earth has been specially designed and created to support life. Modern discoveries have provided wonderful confirmation of this teaching because the earth has been found to have a very sophisticated ecosystem which is ideal for living creatures and plants. Account must be taken that the earth significantly changed at the time of the Fall. In particular, the Bible teaches that there was no death of creatures before the Fall because God called the original creation 'very good' (Genesis 1:31). However, even though the current ecosystem is different to that which existed before the Fall, it still contains clear hallmarks of design. The earth's ecosystem has many interdependent parts that must exist simultaneously for the ecosystem to function properly. This chapter gives a brief survey of some of the sophisticated and irreducible processes that take place in the earth's ecosystem.

3.1 The food chain

The food chain is summarised in Fig. 3–1. The food chain has three main participants: *producers, consumers* and *decomposers*. In general, the producers are plants, the consumers are animals (and humans) and the decomposers are micro-organisms such as bacteria. Each participant in the food chain is dependent on at least one of the other two and therefore plants, animals and micro-organisms must exist simultaneously for the food chain to work.

Plants are generally producers[1] because they manufacture organic food

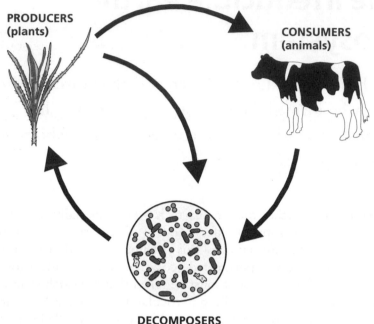

PRODUCERS
(plants)

CONSUMERS
(animals)

DECOMPOSERS
(micro-organisms)

Fig. 3–1 The food chain

through a special process called photosynthesis. Photosynthesis can be summarised as the conversion of carbon dioxide, water and light energy into carbohydrate and oxygen. The carbohydrate that is produced in this process is one of the key constituents of food for animals. Therefore, plants form an essential element in the food chain of animals and the animal kingdom cannot exist without plants. Of course there are a small number of animals that are flesh-eating (carnivores) and can survive by eating other creatures but ultimately there must be many animals in the food chain that are plant-eating (herbivores). Therefore, animals are generally consumers because they rely on the existence of plants.

Even though plants are generally producers, they are still reliant on decomposers. This is because plants require dead animal and plant matter to be decomposed to replenish the soil from which they derive nutrients. One of the most important constituents of soil that has to be replenished is nitrogen because plants use it to make protein. Decomposition can only be carried out by micro-organisms like bacteria and therefore plants cannot exist without bacteria. However, the only source of food for bacteria is in plants and animals. Therefore, animals cannot exist without plants, plants cannot exist without bacteria and bacteria cannot exist without plants and animals!

The food chain shows that there are vital interdependencies between the different types of living organisms on the earth. The food chain is so interdependent that it cannot have evolved but must have been created fully functioning at the beginning of its existence.

3.2 The oxygen, carbon and nitrogen cycles

The oxygen, carbon and nitrogen cycles are summarised in Fig. 3–2 to show that they can only be stable when different creatures and plants exist simultaneously. The air in the earth's atmosphere is made up of the following gases: 78% nitrogen, 21% oxygen, approximately 1% argon and very tiny amounts of carbon dioxide, methane, helium, hydrogen, krypton, neon, ozone and xenon. The earth's ecosystem requires this composition to remain within quite narrow limits in order to sustain life on earth. For

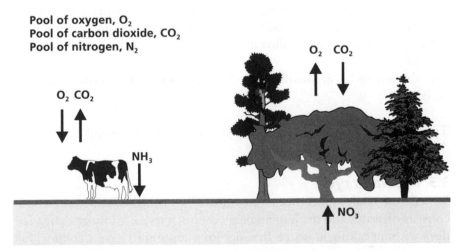

Pool of oxygen, O_2
Pool of carbon dioxide, CO_2
Pool of nitrogen, N_2

Fig. 3–2 The oxygen, carbon and nitrogen cycles

example, even though there is only a tiny amount of carbon dioxide in the air (about 0.03%), if this increases very slightly, then it can lead to damaging effects like global warming. Whilst it is true that increases in carbon dioxide are limited due to the absorption of carbon dioxide by the sea, it has been found that excessive carbon dioxide can also damage sea life such as coral reefs.

Since different types of creatures and plants supply and extract different gases in the atmosphere, it is necessary to have the right balance of these organisms in order to maintain a constant equilibrium. Whereas animals are net consumers of oxygen and generators of carbon dioxide through respiration, plants are net consumers of carbon dioxide and generators of oxygen through photosynthesis.

There is also an interdependent nitrogen cycle. The transfer of nitrogen between the atmosphere and living organisms is shown in Fig. 3-2. When plants and animals die and decay, or when animals excrete, a substance called ammonia is produced. This substance contains nitrogen but not in the right form for plants. However, the metabolic activities (i.e. the living processes) of bacteria convert the ammonia into nitrites and then nitrates that are suitable for plants. Plants can also receive nitrogen directly from the atmosphere if there are particular bacteria living in the plants.

There are other cycles in the earth as well, including the phosphorous and sulphur cycles. Evolutionists admit the fact that animals, plants and bacteria are mutually dependent. For example, a popular textbook on advanced biology says the following about the nitrogen cycle:

The nitrogen cycle...demonstrates the interdependence of animals, plants and bacteria.[2]

The chemical cycles in the earth's ecosystem provide powerful evidence for design.

3.3 The water cycle

Water is of vital importance to creatures. Two thirds of the human body consists of water and the human being cannot survive for more than a few days without taking in water. In order for mankind to have a comfortable existence on the land it is essential to have a clean, local and consistent supply of water. These requirements are very demanding because water can quickly evaporate or become contaminated. Therefore, it is remarkable that most places on the earth do have a convenient supply of clean water through the weather cycle and river systems. Of course, in the modern world the problems caused by pollution mean that there is a need to have additional man-made water delivery systems. However, it is important to appreciate that before the industrial era the natural water supply system was very well suited to the needs of mankind.

The fact that there has been a clean, local and consistent supply of water is remarkable because many complex processes are needed simultaneously to achieve it. Table 3–1 below summarises the main stages and physical processes that take place in the water cycle.

Table 3–1 The water cycle

PHYSICAL PROCESSES	DESCRIPTION
1 Vaporisation	Pure water molecules escape from the sea as clean vapour
2 Buoyancy	Hot air rises taking the vapour to high altitude
3 Condensation	Vapour cools and condenses into water particles to form clouds
4 Precipitation	Water particles collect into heavy droplets
5 Gravity	Water droplets drop to the ground due to gravity
6 Soil permeation	Water seeps through soil and collects under the ground
7 Water pressure	Water builds up pressure underground and ejects from springs
8 Water distribution	Water collects in rivers and lakes and is distributed throughout the land
9 Water use	Water is used by mankind and animals
10 Water recycling	Water flows down rivers back to the sea

Here we see a wonderfully complete water cycle which includes the distribution of clean water throughout the land (Stage 8) and the drainage of dirty water away from the land (Stage 10). In each stage there are many complex processes that take place. For example, precipitation itself requires several sub-processes to take place such as nucleation and surface tension. The fact that all of these processes exist and work together to form an efficient water cycle that is ideal for the needs of mankind gives powerful evidence of design.

UNIQUE PROPERTIES OF WATER

At the atomic level, water is made up of two hydrogen atoms and one oxygen atom. Despite its simple atomic structure, water has some amazing properties that are essential for life on earth. To be of use to life on earth, water must be in the liquid state at room temperature. However, all other substances that have a similar molecular weight and chemical structure to water are not liquid at room temperature. The fact that water is liquid at room temperature is a mystery to scientists.

Like air, water is completely transparent and odourless. These properties of water have several important benefits to people. The fact that water does not smell makes it possible to use water for washing and cooking. The transparency of water is useful for swimming and fishing. Water is also a solvent and can dissolve more substances than any other liquid. This property is extremely important in the life processes of organisms.

Another important and unique property of water is that it expands just before freezing. Like other materials, water shrinks as it decreases in temperature. However, when the temperature drops to 4°C, the shrinking stops and any further reductions in temperature towards freezing cause an expansion of the water. This expansion of water as it approaches freezing point has the effect of making ice less dense than liquid water. The lower density of ice means that it floats on the surface of lakes and seas and insulates the warmer water below. If water behaved like other materials, it would freeze from the bottom up leaving no water in many lakes and seas in wintertime. Without floating ice, a very large proportion of life in lakes and seas would be killed off. The fact that water expands on freezing is another mystery to scientists. However, the special physical properties of water are just what would be expected from a Creator.

3.4 Life-supporting properties of air

Air is critical to all animal and plant life. Creatures breathe air in order to get vital oxygen which is needed to make the cells of the body function. Air actually performs many vital functions and it is wonderful how it is perfectly designed to meet so many different requirements simultaneously. Just some of the functions of air which are important for life on earth include:

I OXYGEN FOR RESPIRATION

All creatures require oxygen for respiration. Air contains about 21% oxygen, which is just right for respiration and life on earth. If there were much less oxygen in the air then this would make animals breathless. However, if there were much more oxygen then fires would burn continuously.

II CARBON DIOXIDE FOR PHOTOSYNTHESIS

All plants require carbon dioxide for photosynthesis.

III NITROGEN FOR PLANTS

All plants need nitrogen and they obtain this from the soil in the form of nitrates. There is a pool of nitrogen in the air which is needed for the nitrogen cycle.

IV RADIATION SCREEN

Air performs a very important function of screening the earth from harmful ultraviolet radiation from the sun. The ozone layer in the atmosphere absorbs the harmful rays before they reach the earth's surface.

V MEDIUM FOR COLOUR

It is easy to take the colour of a blue sky for granted but this could not exist without the special properties of air. For example, from the surface of the moon, the moon's sky appears dark even when the sun is shining. The earth's sky is made blue because air molecules in the earth's atmosphere preferentially scatter shorter wavelength blue light from the white light spectrum of sunlight.

VI MEDIUM FOR SOUND

It is also easy to take sound for granted but this is another essential phenomenon that would not exist without the special properties of air. Air is able to transmit sound by the vibration of the molecules in the air and it does this so precisely that on a still day it is possible to hear sounds from tiny insects and birds.

VII MEDIUM FOR VISION
Air itself is colourless and this makes vision completely clear. Life would be very strange if air had a colour!

VIII MEDIUM FOR SMELL
Air is odourless which means that we are able to sense delicate smells like those of flowers. Life would be very different if air had a smell of its own!

IX MEDIUM FOR THERMAL INSULATION
Air provides thermal insulation. On the moon the temperature is extremely hot in direct sunlight but at night the temperature becomes extremely cold. Air prevents such extreme temperatures by forming an insulating blanket around the earth.

X MEDIUM FOR PRESSURE
Air also provides important pressure. When astronauts are in space, their faces become very puffy because of the lack of air pressure. The air pressure on the earth is just right for keeping the different parts of our bodies in place.

XI DENSITY
Air has just the right level of density to support many important processes. For example, dust particles help to form droplets of rain. One of the reasons why dust is carried up to a high altitude is because air has the right density for dust to be suspended.

XII DRYING
Drying is essential for many animals because it prevents them from getting cold. Creatures dry off after getting wet because water naturally vaporises in the air. This vaporisation involves the conversion of water into an invisible vapour which mixes with the air.

To design a single substance to perform so many complex functions represents a masterpiece of design! Even with man-made products it is not recommended to design for more than one important function because of the difficulties this presents. Yet air is wonderfully designed for at least 12 complex functions which are important for life on earth. The many wonderful properties of air provide powerful evidence of design.

3.5 The Gaia hypothesis

Some biologists have been so impressed with the interdependencies in the earth's ecosystem that they consider the whole planet as one large living organism. People call this the Gaia hypothosis[3] because Gaia in ancient Greek mythology was goddess of the earth. The Gaia hypothesis treats the creation itself as a kind of god that has its own intelligence.

The Gaia hypothesis shows how many modern scientists will do anything to avoid the conclusion of a Creator. The folly of the Gaia hypothesis can be illustrated by analogy with a man-made device. The engine of a motor car presents evidence that a designer was responsible for the order of the system. It would be ridiculous to conclude that the order in this engine gave evidence that the engine itself had the intelligence to build itself. In a similar way, it is ridiculous to suggest that an inanimate earth had such intelligence that it was able to evolve its own ecosystem including living creatures and a biosphere.

3.6 The power and wisdom of God in creation

The first law of thermodynamics states that it is impossible for matter/energy to be created or destroyed. Therefore, whilst it is possible to change energy into matter or matter into energy, the total amount of matter and energy in the universe cannot be changed. A consequence of the first law of thermodynamics is that the very existence of matter/energy is a miracle. The book of Genesis teaches that God made the earth out of nothing. Indeed, God had only to speak commands in order to bring matter and energy into existence. Therefore, the very existence of the huge earth and vast universe demonstrates the power of God. A.W. Pink has described how difficult it is to comprehend God's power and wisdom in creation:

Before man can work he must have both tools and materials, but God began with nothing, and by His word alone out of nothing made all things. The intellect cannot grasp it. God spake and it was done, He commanded and it stood fast (Psalm 33:9).[4]

God's power and wisdom are also seen in the way that He keeps the earth suspended in the right place in the solar system. This aspect of God's power is described in the book of Job: '...He hangs the earth on nothing' (Job 26:7). Of course, scientists say that the earth is simply kept in place by gravity and the movement of the earth around the sun, but gravity is actually a mystery to scientists because no one knows from where it comes or of what it consists. The above statement in the book of Job, even though written thousands of years ago, has been proved to be remarkably true by modern scientific discoveries.

It is also possible to see God's power and wisdom in the weather. This is why Elihu wrote: 'God thunders marvellously with His voice; He does great things which we cannot comprehend. For He says to the snow, "Fall on the earth"... Do you know how the clouds are balanced, those wondrous works of Him who is perfect in knowledge?...With God is awesome majesty. As for the Almighty, we cannot find Him; He is excellent in power, in judgment and abundant justice...' (Job 37:5–23).

Notes on Chapter 3

1 There are actually a tiny number of plants that are both producers and consumers—such as the Venus fly trap—but these are unusual plants and they have a specific ability to exist in nitrogen-deficient places.

2 **Roberts, M.B.V.,** *Biology: a functional approach*, 4th Ed. Nelson, p. 161, 1986.

3 **Myers., N.,** (Editor), *The Gaia atlas of planet management*, Pan Books, p. 13, 1984.

4 **Pink, A.W.,** *The attributes of God*, Baker, pp. 48–49, 1975.

Complete optimum design

As for God, His way is perfect (Psalm 18:30).

One of the most powerful evidences for a Creator is optimum design in nature. Account must be taken of the curse on creation and that this has introduced undesirable effects such as disease and aging. However, despite the effects of the Fall, nature still contains a spectacular level of optimum design which clearly points to a Creator. Many engineers now regard nature as the perfect design handbook and put great efforts into copying nature. This chapter defines complete optimum design and shows how there is remarkable evidence of this hallmark in nature.

4.1 Hallmark of design: complete optimum design

A system has complete optimum design when it has the best mechanisms and materials to fulfil a set of functions and when there are no unnecessary parts. A modern motor car often comes close to achieving complete optimum design. Motor cars have been continuously improved for over one hundred years and car designers have now discovered many of the best mechanisms and materials for fulfilling the functions of a car. In addition, modern motor cars have no superfluous parts. Complete optimum design is so important in engineering that large resources are put into getting the design of products, such as cars, absolutely right.

It is important to clarify that when a system has complete optimum design this does not mean that the performance of every single function is maximised. A system has complete optimum design when the performance of a *group* of functions is maximised. For example, fuel economy and engine power are conflicting functions in automotive engineering and therefore it is impossible to design a car which has the best possible fuel economy at the same time as the most powerful engine. An optimum design of sports car is one which has the best combination of fuel economy and engine power. The fact that a sports car does not have the best possible fuel economy or the best possible power does not disqualify the car from having optimum design.

An intelligent designer is well able to produce complete optimum design in a system by specifying the most appropriate mechanisms and materials and leaving out any unnecessary parts. In contrast, evolution could not achieve complete optimum design because the only objective of evolution is to produce a system which survives. Evolutionists fully agree that if life has evolved by chance, then there should be many examples of non-optimum design or poor design in nature. One reason for this is that some living organisms should be in a state of incomplete adaptation from one environment to another. Another reason for non-optimum design is that if life has evolved by chance, then there should be examples of vestigial organs in nature. Vestigial organs are organs that supposedly had a useful function in an evolutionary ancestor but now have no useful function.

4.2 Complete optimum design in nature

Modern studies have revealed that living organisms throughout nature are extremely well designed for their environment. Books on nature are full of explanations of how organisms are well designed.[1] In addition, there is virtually no mention of any non-optimum or poor design. Evolutionists have tried in vain to find examples of poor design in nature in order to support the theory of evolution but they have failed. In the few cases where evolutionary scientists have claimed to have found poor design, it has actually been found that the only poor thing was the understanding of these scientists about what a good design actually was! The continuous praise given to design in nature is a great evidence for a Creator.

BIRDS

Birds provide an excellent example of complete optimum design. There are about 9,000 different species of bird living today and all of them are supremely well designed for their particular environment. One of the optimum design features of birds is the feather. In the case of flying birds, the flight feathers always have the intricate interlocking of barbs and barbules. But if birds had evolved, we would not expect to see every single species of bird with an optimum feather design. Since evolution would require millions of years for a feather to become fully optimised for flight, we would expect to see some flying creatures today with feathers which were not yet fully optimised. However, no such creatures exist and no such creatures are present in the fossil record. It is very difficult for evolution to explain why there was supposedly once a need for land creatures to fly but that the need is no longer present. It is also very difficult for evolution to explain why there is no trace of evidence that land creatures ever evolved into birds. The optimum design of birds provides remarkable evidence of design.

THE WANDERING ALBATROSS

Albatrosses are a type of seabird which can be found from the Antarctic to the northern oceans. Albatrosses have a stocky body, webbed feet, very long wings and a hooked bill. They also have specialised mechanisms for navigating, finding food and storing food. A picture of an albatross is shown in Fig. 4–1. The albatross glides above the open seas, occasionally coming down to the surface to feed on food such as squid, fish and krill. There are about 24 living species of albatross although different bird books quote different numbers because biologists do not agree on how to define individual species. Also, the number of species may drop because several species are endangered and could become extinct in the near future.

The largest albatrosses (which are sometimes called the great albatrosses) are the wandering albatross, royal albatross and Amsterdam albatross. The wandering albatross has a wingspan of up to 3.5m which is the largest of any living bird. Most of the large albatross species, such as the wandering albatross, live in the southern oceans where the windy conditions are ideal for large gliders.

Fig. 4–1 An albatross

All albatross species are supremely well designed for their respective environments. However, the gigantic size of the wandering albatross makes it a particularly interesting example of complete optimum design. Aeronautical engineers have calculated the optimum layout of a glider and it has a remarkable resemblance to the shape of a wandering albatross with very long slender wings. Amazingly, a wandering albatross may spend weeks in the air before landing on the sea and it may spend two years at sea before returning to land to breed. A wandering albatross typically flies hundreds of thousands of kilometres in its lifetime.

Some people have argued that the wandering albatross has a design weakness in that it struggles to take off from the ground. When taking off, the wandering albatross is commonly observed to require a very long run-up and to put great effort into flapping its wings. However, even though the wandering albatross does struggle to get off the ground, it would be entirely wrong to call this a design weakness. The reason for this is that the wandering albatross must have a superb glider design in order to glide for vast distances across the oceans. When all the multiple functions of the albatross are considered, it is clear that the wandering albatross has an ideal design for its environment. It would be physically impossible for a bird with a 3.5m wing span to take off in the way that a small bird does, so it cannot be argued that the wandering albatross has a design weakness in this respect. The fact that the wandering albatross is able to take off even though it is essentially a gliding bird only adds to the wonder of its design.

The optimum design of the wandering albatross can also be illustrated by analogy with a large aircraft like a passenger jet. Some passenger jets are very large and require a very long runway in order to obtain sufficient speed for take-off. It would be wrong to label a large passenger aircraft as a sub-optimal design just because it requires more runway than a smaller plane. In a similar way, it would be wrong to say that a wandering albatross has a sub-optimal design because it requires a relatively long run-up.

4.3 Optimum design in mosaic creatures

There are some creatures which possess an unusual combination of features which are usually associated with different groups of creature. The mixture of features has resulted in the label of 'mosaic' creatures. Some of the most famous examples are Archaeopteryx, Ichthyostega and the platypus. The first two of these are extinct but the platypus is still living. Archaeopteryx is an extinct bird which had some features normally associated with reptiles such as teeth and wing claws. Ichthyostega is an extinct land vertebrate which had some features normally associated with fish such as paddle-shaped limbs. The platypus is a mammal which has some features normally associated with reptiles such as egg laying.

Evolutionists often claim that mosaic creatures are an example of intermediate forms of creatures. However, such claims are false because there is nothing intermediate about the 'features' of mosaic creatures. For example, Archaeopteryx is claimed to be an intermediate between reptiles and birds. But as mentioned in Chapter 2, Archaeopteryx had flight feathers which are identical to the flight feathers of modern birds and Archaeopteryx was as well designed for flight as any modern bird. Since Archaeopteryx was perfectly designed for flight, it must be concluded that it was not an intermediate creature. The fact that Archaeopteryx contained some unusual features such as teeth and wing claws does not change the fact that Archaeopteryx was a bird.

Evolutionists also claim that Ichthyostega is an intermediate form between fish and land animals. However, when the environment of Ichthyostega is taken into consideration, it becomes clear that there is actually nothing intermediate about the features of Ichthyostega. Ichthyostega lived in shallow water and so the best design for that creature was to have a land vertebrate structure with some features for paddling in water. The fact that it had features which were suited to shallow water does not change the fact that it was a land vertebrate. There is an interesting analogy between the features of Ichthyostega and the features of ducks. The fact that ducks have webbed-feet for paddling does not make them intermediate between fish and birds! In a similar way, the fact that Ichthyostega had limbs for paddling does not mean that it was intermediate between fish and land creatures.

When account is taken of the environment in which Archaeopteryx, Ichthyostega or the platypus lived or live, it becomes clear that they represent complete optimum design and that there is nothing intermediate about their features. The presence of mosaic creatures is entirely consistent with a wise Creator who wanted to fill all the different environments of the earth with creatures. An excellent discussion about the absence of intermediates between fish and tetrapods (four-limbed animals) has been produced by Garner.[2]

4.4 Absence of vestigial parts

If evolution had occurred, there would be many strange vestigial parts in creatures today. In particular, one would expect to see many vestigial parts in the human being because, according to evolutionary theory, the human being has a great number of ancestors. Such a large number of ancestors would contain a vast range of organs and characteristics and many organs that had previously been useful would inevitably become functionless. According to evolution, vestigial organs could only be removed if there was a selective advantage in them being removed. For example, if a vestigial organ was large or heavy, it could be advantageous for the creature if the organ was lost. Since vestigial organs could theoretically come in any size, one would expect to see many small vestigial organs in humans today.

One of the most obvious vestigial parts that humans should have is body fur, since all of our supposed recent ancestors had fur. According to evolution, the only way that humans could have lost fur was if there had been a selective advantage in it being lost. However, from a survival point of view, there are actually definite advantages in having fur. The fact that humans need to wear clothes in the vast majority of places in the world shows that humans normally have need of clothing. It is very difficult for evolution to explain why human beings have no fur. Indeed, it is also very difficult for evolution to explain why there are absolutely no ape-like vestigial features in humans.

Since Darwin first published the theory of evolution, much effort has gone into searching for vestigial organs in humans. This search has been very disappointing for evolutionists for a number of reasons. Firstly, rather than finding hundreds of clear examples of vestigial organs, evolutionists have found only a few very disputable examples. Secondly, over the last 100 years the claimed list has been reduced drastically to only a few because it has been found that most of the organs that were thought to be vestigial actually have important functions. Thirdly, our understanding of the human being is still so incomplete that it is almost certain that functions will be identified for the remaining so-called vestigial organs.

Examples of currently disputed vestigial organs include the small coccyx bone at the base of the spine and wisdom teeth. The coccyx bone is claimed by evolutionists to be a relic of a tailbone. However, without the coccyx it can be very difficult to sit, so it cannot be considered to be a functionless relic of a tailbone. Wisdom teeth are claimed by evolutionists to cause problems because according to evolution, the jaw became smaller leaving less room for teeth. However, modern studies have shown that most problems with wisdom teeth are not related to jaw size.[3]

In recent years there have been some claims that the human genome (genetic code) contains large sections of vestigial DNA. Only 3–5% of the human genome contains DNA that is known to specify proteins and encode for RNAs. (Proteins are building block materials of the body and RNAs are molecules which read information on DNA). Since over 95% of the genome appears not to be involved with producing proteins, some evolutionists have claimed that this section of the genome contains vestigial or 'junk' DNA. However, scientists are now discovering that some sections of DNA which were previously described as junk have actually been found to perform important functions. These functions include such things as the regulation of developmental changes in the embryo during growth and the control of structural changes to the DNA molecule during the functioning of the cell. It is also likely that there is some degenerate DNA which has appeared due to gene mutations, which are part of the general decay of nature which has taken place since the Fall. Therefore, there is absolutely no reason to view unidentified DNA as vestigial DNA. Nancy Darrall has produced an excellent review of the current understanding of DNA.[4]

4.5 Superior design in nature

According to evolution, nature should contain inferior designs to man's designs because man can bring parts together simultaneously whereas evolution is limited to incremental change. This fact is fully acknowledged by evolutionists. For example, a leading modern-day evolutionist, Steven Vogel, has said:

...the evolutionary process faces constraints far more severe than anything impeding human designers. We biologists recognise these constraints, but we don't often rise above our natural chauvinism and make enough noise about them. Every organism must grow from an initially smaller to an ultimately larger size. Nature in effect must transmute a motorcycle into an automobile while providing continuous transportation. The need for growth without loss of function can impose severe geometrical limitations.[5]

Vogel rightly points out that evolution is far more constrained than intelligent design because all intermediate mechanisms must provide continuous functions. It is interesting to note that Vogel acknowledges that biologists do not admit the limitations of evolution as much as they should. It is almost certain that biologists do not make this admission because they can see that there is a contradiction between the limitation of evolution and supreme design in nature. If the general public realised that the process of evolution is severely restricted, then they would be much more likely to reject evolution as a credible explanation of origins.

Modern studies have shown that the mechanisms found in nature are always superior to man-made products. A comparison between the human heart and a man-made pump can illustrate the superiority of natural mechanisms. The human heart can function as a self-maintaining pump for 75 years or more. During this time it beats around 2.5 billion times and pumps more than 150 million litres of blood around the body.[6] This performance is vastly superior to any man-made pump working in similar conditions. Also, it is very difficult to design a man-made replacement heart with anywhere near the same capability as a living heart.

The superior design of natural systems is demonstrated by the fact that there is a constant desire by engineers to copy nature. The practice of copying designs from nature is called 'biomimetics', which means the mimicking of biological systems. The subject is now so popular in industry that it is taught to undergraduate engineers. I currently teach and research the subject of biomimetics at Bristol University. One of the main reasons for the recent upsurge in interest in this area is that technology is now so complex and expensive to develop that there are great advantages in copying optimum designs in nature.

It is very significant that in biomimetics there is always the assumption that the natural world contains complete optimum design. Engineering scientists also make an assumption that nature contains far better designs than those of human designers. One engineering journal recently described the supreme quality of design in nature and made the following prediction:

It will be Mother Nature who will be the real victor in the high tech, digitised battlespace of 21st century [design] warfare.[7]

There are many examples of mechanisms in nature which have been copied by design engineers. Velcro is a very common method of fastening and this idea was inspired by the burr plant. Hexagonal cells are a very important type of structural layout in engineering and this was inspired by the bees' honeycomb. It is likely that the tail feathers of birds helped inspire the Wright brothers to design the first tail-fin rudder on an aircraft.

At present, some advanced engineering materials and mechanisms are being developed based on designs found in nature. The following list shows a few examples of natural mechanisms which have recently been copied or which are currently being studied with a view to being copied:

NATURAL MECHANISM	MAN-MADE COPY
Plant microstructure	Structural material[8]
Human skull	Helmet[9]
Fish slime	Polymers for drag reduction[10]
Shark scales	Surface profile for drag reduction[11]
Down feathers	Insulation[12]
Reliability strategies	Reliability strategies in process plants[13]
Plant deployment	Spacecraft deployment mechanisms[14]
Human limb	Deployment systems[15]

It is very difficult for the evolutionist to explain how, on the one hand, the supposed process of evolution is severely restricted compared to intelligent design but, on the other hand, nature contains designs that are far more advanced than those produced by human designers!

4.6 Great scientists who believed in complete optimum design

The great scientist Leonardo da Vinci was a firm believer in a Creator. Having spent much time as a scientist and engineer, he had no doubt that there was complete optimum design in nature. He wrote:

Although human genius through various inventions makes instruments corresponding to the same ends, it will never discover an invention more beautiful, nor more ready nor more economical than does nature, because in her inventions nothing is lacking, and nothing is superfluous.[16]

Louis Pasteur was another great scientist who believed in a Creator. He wrote:

The more I study nature, the more I stand amazed at the work of the Creator.[17]

If evolution were true, then these statements by Leonardo da Vinci and Louis Pasteur would not be correct because evolution would inevitably produce vestigial parts and sub-optimal designs. However, modern studies have proved these statements to be remarkably correct.

4.7 Modern atheistic philosophy

Modern books and television programmes on nature repeatedly talk of the wonder of living organisms. They say that nature performs this clever process and that nature has found this sophisticated mechanism. However, there is never any mention of the Creator who made those processes and mechanisms. Readers and viewers are given the impression that nature itself has designed living organisms. The modern education system also teaches children that there is no need to believe in a Creator. By teaching children that there is no need for a Designer, the education system is effectively promoting atheism.

The rejection of a Creator by modern man is totally unjustified and totally wrong. God is the Creator of all the wonderful designs found in nature. In the same way that every detail of a car has been designed, so every detail of nature has been consciously designed. In the case of the bird feather, every single barb and barbule has been deliberately put in place in order to produce a structure that is supremely well designed for flight and beauty. In a similar way, every other detail of nature has been consciously designed.

4.8 The power and wisdom of God in creation

The fact that nature contains optimum designs that are vastly superior to the best human designs shows that nature has a Designer who is vastly superior to human designers. The fact that God only needed to speak a command in order to bring organisms into existence shows that God is infinitely more powerful than human designers. The complete optimum design found in nature bears witness to the power and wisdom of God. The psalmist was well aware of God's power and wisdom when he wrote: 'Great is our Lord, and mighty in power; His understanding is infinite.' (Psalm 147:5).

Notes on Chapter 4

1   **Thompson, D.,** *On growth and form*, Cambridge University Press, p. 236, 1961.

2   **Garner, P.,** *Did fish give rise to the tetrapods?*, Creation Science Movement, Pamphlet Number 336, 2001.

3   **Bergman, J.,** 'Are wisdom teeth vestiges of human evolution?', *Creation ex Nihilo*, Vol. 12, No. 3, pp. 297–304, 1998.

4   **Darrall, N.M.,** *Junk DNA—more vestigial organs*, Origins, No. 29, pp. 2–13, November 2000.

5   **Vogel, S.,** *Cats' paws and catapults*, Penguin, p. 23, 1998.

6   **Roberts, M.B.V.,** *Biology a functional approach*, 4th Ed, Nelson, p. 170, 1986.

7   **Dunn., J.,** *Materials*, Professional Engineering, pp. 20–21, 15th October 1997.

8   **Karam, G.N. and Gibson, L.J.,** 'Biomimicking of animal quills and plant stems—Natural cylindrical shells with foam cores', *Materials Science Engineering C—Biomim* 2: (1–2) 113–132, 1994.

9   **Shelley, T.,** 'Movable layers prevents head injuries', *Eureka on Campus*, pp. 32–33, Summer 1999.

10 **Vogel, S.,** *op.cit.*, p. 278.

11 **Vogel, S.,** *op.cit.*, p. 279.

12 **Bonser R.H.C. and Dawson, C.,** 'The structural mechanical properties of down feathers and biomimicking natural insulation materials', *J Materials Science Letters* 18: (21) 1769–1770, 1999.

13 **Burgess, S.C.,** *op. cit.*

14 **Vincent, J.F.V.,** 'Deployable structures in nature: potential for biomimicking', *Proc. Instn Mech. Engrs,* Vol. 214 Part C, pp. 1–10, 2000.

15 **Burgess, S.C.,** 'Polar Platform Primary Deployment Mechanism', *Fifth European space mechanism and tribology symposium,* ESTEC, Noordwijk, The Netherlands, October 1992, pp. 285–289.

16 **Da Vinci, L.,** Manuscript RL 19115v; K/P 114r located in the Royal Library, Windsor Castle, Windsor, England, ca. 1500.

17 **Lamont, A.,** *21 Great Scientists who believed,* Creation Science Foundation, p. 143, 1995.

Added beauty in the peacock tail

He has made everything beautiful in its time
(Ecclesiastes 3:11).

One of the most positive evidences for a Creator is the existence of profound beauty throughout the natural world. Beauty is a particularly strong evidence of design when beauty has been added to an object for the sake of producing beauty. This chapter defines added beauty and describes why the peacock tail provides spectacular evidence of this type of beauty.[1]

5.1 Hallmark of design: added beauty

Beauty can be perceived through any of the five senses of sight, hearing, touch, smell and taste. Beauty in appearance is produced by attributes such as patterns, brightness, variety, curves, blending or any combination of such attributes. These attributes are very real attributes. Therefore, even though beauty cannot be quantified, beauty is a very real thing. The fact that the Bible specifically mentions beauty on many occasions confirms that beauty is indeed a real property. Beauty is so important in engineering design that there is a whole subject called *aesthetics* which defines how beauty can be added to man-made products.[2]

INHERENT BEAUTY AND ADDED BEAUTY

An object can have two types of beauty: inherent beauty and added beauty. Inherent beauty is a beauty that exists as a by-product of mechanical design. In contrast, added beauty is a type of beauty which has the sole purpose of providing a beautiful display. These two types of beauty can be seen in man-made products like buildings and bridges. An example of inherent beauty is found in the shape of a suspension bridge. A suspension bridge has a curved cable structure because this is an efficient way of supporting a roadway. However, the end result can be a very elegant and beautiful design.

An example of added beauty can be seen in the decoration of a classical column. The classical column shown in Fig. 5–1(a) has an elaborate form with intricate carvings and grooves. There is no mechanical reason for a classical column to be any more than a plain cylinder, like the one shown in Fig. 5–1(b), yet the designers embellish the column with elaborate patterns just for the sake of adding beauty. When added beauty is seen in man-made or natural objects, this represents very strong evidence for design because there is no mechanical reason for the beautiful appearance.

Evolutionists fully admit that there are features in nature whose only purpose is to produce a beautiful effect. Charles Darwin said this about the beauty of male creatures like the peacock:

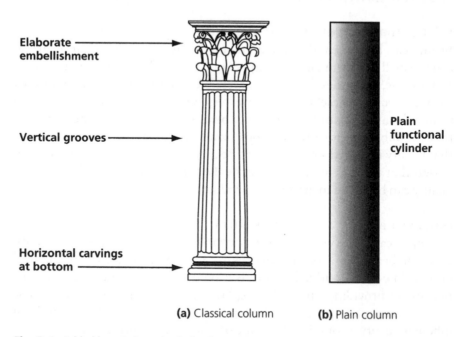

Elaborate embellishment

Vertical grooves

Plain functional cylinder

Horizontal carvings at bottom

(a) Classical column   **(b)** Plain column

Fig. 5–1 Added beauty in a classical column

A great number of male animals… have been rendered beautiful for beauty's sake; the most refined beauty may serve as a charm for the female, and for no other purpose; that ornament and variety is the sole object, I have myself but little doubt.[3]

Evolutionists claim that the theory of sexual selection can fully explain the existence of added beauty in nature. However, the theory of sexual selection is incapable of explaining the profound and subtle levels of beauty that exist in natural objects such as the peacock tail. At the end of this chapter there is a section explaining some of the major problems with the theory of sexual selection.

5.2 The peacock tail

Most species of bird have two types of tail feather: flight feathers and tail-coverts. The flight feathers provide stability during flight, while the tail-coverts cover and protect the tail region of the bird. In the vast majority of birds, the tail-coverts are small feathers just a few centimetres long. However, some birds like the peacock have very large tail-coverts for decorative purposes. (It should be noted that a peacock is a male peafowl whilst a peahen is a female peafowl.) Evolutionists fully agree that the only purpose of the peacock tail feathers is to attract females.[4] During the breeding season, the peacock will often display his tail feathers in an attempt to woo a peahen. The reason why it is generally the male that has a beautiful coloration is that the female must spend long periods on the nest and therefore must be well camouflaged.

The peacock tail feathers are sometimes called decorative or ornamental feathers but most people refer to them simply as the peacock tail feathers. An adult peacock has an average of 200 tail feathers and these are shed and re-grown annually. Of the 200 or so feathers, about 170 are 'eye' feathers and 30 are 'T' feathers. The 'eyes' are sometimes referred to as ocellations. The length of the feathers varies from a few centimetres to over 1.5 m. The peacock tail feathers are some of the longest and most brilliantly coloured feathers in nature. The unique length and structure of the peacock tail feathers is acknowledged by bird experts.[5,6]

5.3 The beauty of the peacock display

When a peacock displays his tail feathers, a magnificent 'fan formation' of feathers forms a beautiful backdrop to the body of the peacock, as shown on the front cover of this book. To produce this fan-like arrangement, the feathers must be very accurately aligned. Another remarkable feature of the displayed feathers is that they are 'deployed' into position by muscles in the peacock's tail. Not only can the peacock deploy the feathers, but he can also make them vibrate and produce a characteristic hum. Another beautiful feature of the displayed feathers is that the eye feathers are spaced apart with a remarkable degree of uniformity. All the eyes are visible because the feathers are layered with the short feathers at the front and the longer feathers at the back.

The eye and T feathers have complimentary shapes because the T feathers have a profile which is the inverse of the shape of the eye feathers, as shown in Fig. 5–2. Each individual eye feather and T feather is an object of outstanding

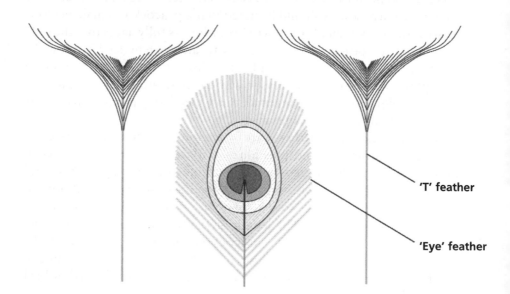

'T' feather

'Eye' feather

Fig. 5–2 'T' and 'Eye' feathers in the peacock tail

beauty in itself. The eye feathers contain beautiful patterns with brilliant colours, whilst the T feathers form a beautiful border to the fan.

5.4 The structure of the peacock tail feathers

The basic structure of the peacock tail feather in the eye region is shown in Fig. 5–3(a). For comparison, the structure of a typical flight feather is shown in Fig. 5–3(b). Like the flight feather, the peacock tail feather has a central stem with an array of barbs on each side. In addition, these barbs are covered with a large number of barbules. A large peacock eye feather may contain up to 300 barbs and one million barbules.

Even though there is a basic similarity with a flight feather, the peacock tail feather has an unusual overlapping barbule structure. The barbules are like long segmented ribbons which overlap to form a smooth surface on top of the barbs. (Under a microscope the barbules are slightly curved and the surface has a bubbly appearance.) Each barbule generally contains at least

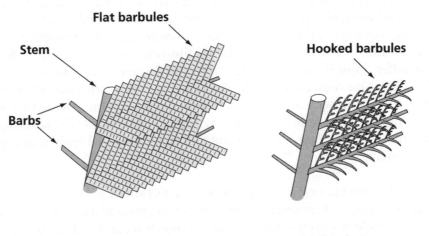

(a) Peacock tail feather   (b) Flight feather

Fig. 5–3 Feather structure

20 separate segments. Since a large peacock feather contains up to one million barbules, there may be around 20 million barbule segments in a large peacock feather!

5.5 Optical colours in the peacock tail feathers

The colours in the peacock tail are not pigment colours but structural colours which are produced by an optical effect called thin-film interference.7 The thin-film interference takes place in the transparent segments of the barbules and produces bright and iridescent colours. An iridescent colour is a colour that changes with the angle of view. The barbules are dark purple in the 'pupil' of the eye, blue in the 'iris' of the eye, bronze around the iris and green on the fringes. Away from the eye region, the barbules are uniformly green.

BACKGROUND TO THIN-FILM INTERFERENCE

Thin-film interference can be produced in one or more layers of a very thin and transparent material. Usually the thin film is placed on a dark surface. The thickness of the transparent material must be close to the wavelengths of visible light. Visible colours have wavelengths of between 0.4μ and 0.8μ and thin films typically have a thickness of between 0.3μ and 1.5μ (μ = one micron which is one thousandth of one millimetre!). Another requirement for thin-film interference is that the thin film must have a refractive index that differs from air (so that the light is retarded when it passes through the thin film). One common example of where thin-film interference occurs is in oil slicks on a wet road. When a car spills drops of oil on a wet road, the oil will often form a thin layer on the wet surface of the road. The resulting thin film produces blue and green colours even though oil itself is nearly transparent.

THIN-FILM INTERFERENCE IN THE PEACOCK BARBULES

In the peacock tail feathers, thin-film interference takes place in three layers of keratin which surround the barbules, as shown in Fig. 5–4. Each barbule is about 60μ wide and 5μ thick.[8] The foam core is 2μ thick and the keratin layers are extremely thin, being about 0.4–0.5μ thick.[9] Other types of birds, such as hummingbirds, pigeons and kingfishers, have some patches of flat iridescent barbules, but the peacock has the largest iridescent barbules of any known bird.[10] The colours in the eye feather can only be seen on the front surface of the feather because this is where the barbules are positioned. The back of the feather is uniformly brown because the barbs contain a brown pigment.

The principle of thin-film interference in a single layer of keratin is shown in Fig. 5–4. White light is reflected off the front and back surfaces of the thin film. The light which passes through the keratin is retarded (slows down) whereas the light which reflects off the front surface is not. Therefore, some of the colour components of white light which are reflected from the back surface become out of phase with the corresponding light-waves which are reflected off the front surface. When two wave trains of the same colour are out of phase, this causes destructive interference to take place and the colour is removed. In the case of white light hitting a thin film, the result of the interference is a reflected colour due to the remaining colour components of white light. In practice, interference occurs simultaneously in all three thin films.

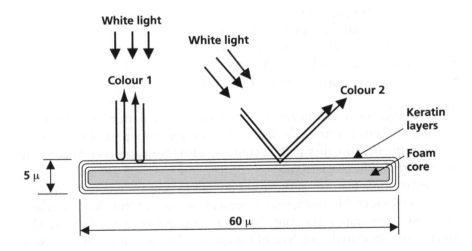

Fig. 5–4 Cross-section of a single tail feather barbule

OPTIMUM DESIGN IN THE BARBULES

The barbules in the peacock feather contain an amazing degree of optimum design. The thicknesses of the keratin layers are optimal for producing the brightest thin-film colours. The different colours in the eye pattern are the result of minute changes in the depth of thickness of the keratin layers.[11] In order to produce a particular colour, the keratin thickness must be accurate to within about 0.05μ (one twenty thousandth of one millimetre!). The dark brown background colouring of the barbs is optimal because it prevents light shining through the back of the feather. The three layers add to the brilliance of the colours in the feather by adding multiple components of light. A further optimum feature in thin-film design is that the barbules are slightly curved in the longitudinal direction.[12] This curvature causes a mingling of slightly different colours and results in a softening of the colours seen in the keratin layers.

5.6 The beauty of the eye feather

Fig. 5–5 shows a picture of the top section of the peacock eye feather. There are several beautiful features to the feather:

- Bright colours
- Intricate eye pattern
- Loose barbs below the eye pattern
- Absence of stem in top half of eye pattern
- Narrow stem in bottom half of eye pattern
- Brown coating of stem near the eye pattern

The bright colours and intricate shapes of the eye pattern are the most striking aesthetic features. The loose barbs on the lower part of the feather are beautiful because they make a contrast with the neatness and precision of the barbs in the eye pattern.

The last three features in the list above are usually only noticed by very careful observers. However, they represent important 'finishing touches' which make an important contribution to the beauty of the feather. The absence of a stem in the top half of the eye is an important detail because it prevents the pattern from being completely divided into two sections. The stem is able to be absent because the barbs gradually change in their angle

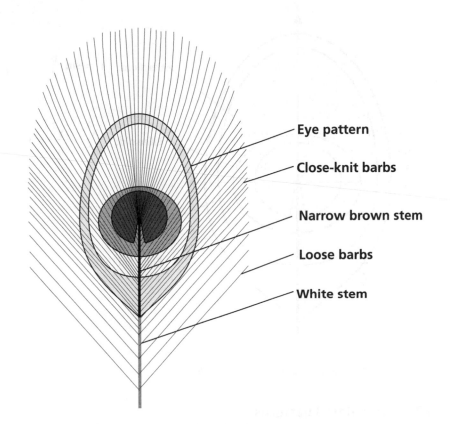

Eye pattern

Close-knit barbs

Narrow brown stem

Loose barbs

White stem

Fig. 5–5 Features of the eye feather

of orientation and fan out right around the top of the feather, as shown in Fig. 5–5. The narrowness of the stem in the bottom half of the eye pattern is important because this makes the stem fairly obscure. The brown coating of the stem in the area of the eye pattern is important because the stem is a natural white colour and this would be too conspicuous in the eye pattern. It is interesting to note that the stem is white everywhere except local to the eye pattern. This demonstrates that the brown coating near the eye pattern is a deliberate feature.

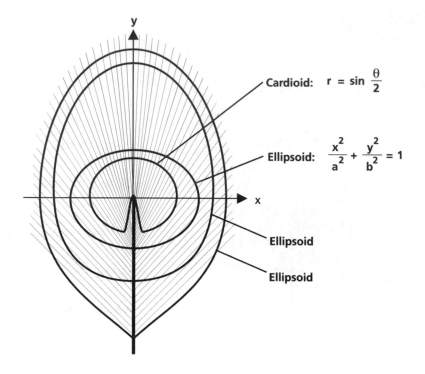

Cardioid: $r = \sin \dfrac{\theta}{2}$

Ellipsoid: $\dfrac{x^2}{a^2} + \dfrac{y^2}{b^2} = 1$

Ellipsoid

Ellipsoid

Fig. 5–6 Mathematical curves in the eye pattern

5.7 Precise digital patterns

The eye feather contains remarkably precise patterns. The eye pattern is made up of rounded shapes that have a high degree of resolution, as shown in Fig. 5–6. The 'pupil' of the eye is a dark purple cardioid shape and the 'iris' is a blue ellipsoid shape. These shapes are located within a pointed bronze ellipsoid which is surrounded by one or two green fringes. A very important feature of the eye pattern is that it is a 'digital' pattern which is formed by the combined effect of many thousands of individual barbule segments. Some patterns in nature are formed by natural growth mechanisms, as with the spiral shape of the nautilus shell. However, the eye pattern in the peacock tail requires the precise co-ordination of independent barbules and this cannot be achieved by a simple growth mechanism.

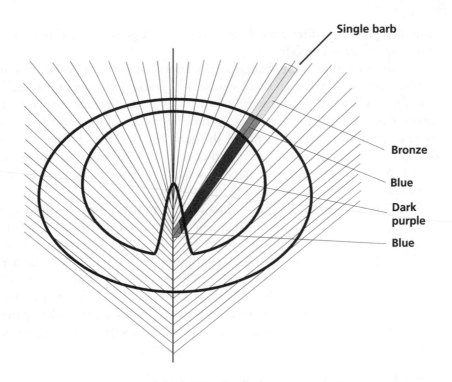

Single barb

Bronze

Blue

Dark purple

Blue

Fig. 5–7  Colour changes on one barb

The way that barbules and barbule segments on adjacent barbs co-ordinate perfectly with each other to produce the eye pattern is amazing. On each side of the eye pattern every single barb has a unique sequence and spacing of colours along its length. Yet all the barbs co-ordinate with great precision to produce the eye pattern. The changes of colour along the length of one barb are shown in Fig. 5–7. Along the length of the barb there are abrupt and minute changes in the thickness of the keratin films so that different thin-film colours are produced. The thin-film colours change from blue to dark purple then back to blue and then to bronze. The colours on the barb match the colours of adjacent barbs so that the eye pattern is formed. Observations under a microscope indicate that an individual barbule segment always has one colour but that a single barbule can contain segments of different colours if the barbule goes across a boundary from one colour to another.

The abrupt nature of the changes in thickness is important because if the changes were gradual, then there would be a gradual change in colour.[13] The abrupt change in thickness of keratin is an amazing feature because it involves a sudden and precise change in the dimensions of the barbule. Even more amazingly, along the length of the barb, the thickness of the keratin does not continually get thicker and thicker (or thinner and thinner) but it both increases and decreases in thickness. Such directional changes cannot be produced by simple growth mechanisms.

Since each barbule segment produces one colour, the resolution of the pattern is equal to the size of one segment, which is about 60μ square. This is equivalent to a resolution of about 280 dots-per-inch which is comparable to modern printing technology! A large peacock feather contains over 100 barbs in the eye region. The number of barbules in the eye pattern is the order of one hundred thousand. Since each barb contains about 20 segments, the number of individual segments which make up the eye pattern is about 2 million. These 2 million segments produce a wonderfully precise pattern!

5.8 Information content in the genetic code

The genetic code of a peacock must contain all the information that is necessary to produce the eye pattern in the tail feathers. To specify the pattern, there must be timing or positional instructions which cause exactly the right thickness of keratin to be grown on every individual segment of every single barbule. Since the tail feathers have very complicated structures and colour-producing mechanisms, there must be a very large amount of design information in the genetic code.

It is very difficult to determine how many genes are required to specify the aesthetic features of a peacock tail feather because the formation of patterns on feathers is not at all well understood by scientists. When a feather grows, it has been found that cells are able to rhythmically switch colour-producing pigments on and off. This process is known to produce the bars on striped feathers.[14] In the same way that pigments are switched on and off, it may be that the thickness of thin films can be switched on and off to produce bars on iridescent feathers. However, such a switching process cannot explain how a complex pattern can be produced. At present, scientists do not understand how complex patterns, like the peacock eye, are formed.

A conservative estimate of the information required for the eye pattern can be made by assuming that each separate aesthetic feature is specified by one gene. By assuming that each colour and each shape within the eye pattern represents a separate feature, and taking into account the other features discussed in this chapter, the total number of aesthetic features in a single feather comes to about 20. Therefore, a conservative estimate of the number of genes required for the peacock tail is about 20. In practice, this may be a very conservative estimate. In particular, it may be that many genes are required to produce each shape in the eye pattern since the eye pattern is formed from the co-ordinated arrangement of over 100 barbs. In addition, the fanning-out of barbs in the top of the feather, where there is no stem, is a complex feature that may well require several genes for its production.

Even if it is assumed that only 20 genes are required to specify the beautiful features of the peacock tail, this still amounts to a great deal of genetic information. A gene typically consists of several hundred chemical units of information. Therefore, 20 genes would contain many thousands of chemical units of information. According to evolution, all of this information has appeared gradually by genetic mistakes and by a process of sexual selection. However, as will be shown later, there are immense problems with the theory of sexual selection.

5.9 The purpose of beauty in the peacock tail

The beauty of the peacock tail is so profound that it must be concluded that the *main* purpose of the beauty is to give pleasure to the Creator and to man. This conclusion is totally rejected by evolutionists. Evolutionists argue that since the peacock tail is used to attract peahens, this must mean that the beauty does not exist for man. However, there is no logic to this argument. Just because the peacock tail is used to attract peahens, this does not rule out the possibility that the main purpose of the peacock tail is to bring pleasure to man. In fact, there are at least two very logical reasons why the Creator would give the peacock feathers a role in the courtship ritual.

A TRIGGER FOR DISPLAYS

If the peacock did not have to display its feathers to attract a peahen, then the tail feathers might not ever be displayed. By giving the peacock a need to display his tail feathers, this ensures that the feathers are often displayed for the enjoyment of man. Not only is the courtship ritual a clever way of producing frequent displays but it is also an appropriate trigger because courtship itself is a beautiful process.

CONSERVATION OF BEAUTY

Another benefit of the courtship ritual is that it may be helping to conserve the beauty of the peacock tail feathers. If feathers were not needed for attracting females, then the peacock could find it a great advantage if it lost the tail feathers due to gene mutations. The reason for this is that the tail feathers make the peacock slow and conspicuous and easier to catch by predators. This is an example of where a 'loss' of information in the genetic code would be a great advantage in terms of survival. (A loss of information in the genetic code is not an example of evolution.) However, since the tail feathers do play an important functional role, it is not an advantage for the peacock to lose its tail feathers. Any peacock which lost its tail feathers would find that it could escape from predators more quickly, but it would also find it harder to attract a mate. Therefore, the courtship ritual is a clever means of preserving the beauty of the peacock tail.

The courtship ritual is so useful for triggering displays and conserving beauty that it actually adds weight to the argument that the peacock tail has been made for the pleasure of man. The evolutionary argument that the courtship ritual rules out man-centred purpose has no justification.

5.10 The theory of sexual selection

The theory of sexual selection was first proposed by Charles Darwin in his book *The Descent of Man*[15] and is now generally accepted by evolutionists.[16] According to the theory of sexual selection, when females have a preference for beautiful males, beautiful males will be more successful at producing offspring, and so males will gradually become more beautiful over time. Evolutionists fully recognise that a female such as a peahen does not have aesthetic appreciation and that the preference of the female must be based on an instinctive response. In addition, it is recognised that the instinctive response needs to be specified by one or more genes in the genetic code. These genes are called *preference* genes. For sexual selection to work, there must be a preference gene in the female for every single beautiful feature in the male. In addition, there must be a *trait* gene in the male for every single one of his beautiful features. According to the theory of evolution, all of these genes have been produced by random genetic mistakes.

A key aspect of the theory of sexual selection is that survivability is not measured in ability to escape from predators but in ability to produce offspring. Evolutionists fully recognise that sexual selection would generally produce features that reduce ability to escape from predators because aesthetic features generally make a creature more conspicuous and slower. However, according to evolution, if females prefer beautiful males for mating (and if they are able to choose who they mate with!), then the advantage of beauty outweighs the advantages of camouflage and manoeuvrability. According to the theory of sexual selection, decorative features such as the peacock tail will develop to the point at which the disadvantages of being caught by a predator outweigh the advantages of being selected by a female.[17]

At present, there is no conclusive evidence about the existence of preference genes in females. If future experiments show that there are no preference genes in the peahen, then the theory of sexual selection will absolutely collapse. However, even if there are preference genes for aesthetic features, this does not prove that the sexual selection theory is correct. As explained earlier, a Creator could well have used preference genes as a means of 'maintaining' beautiful features. The presence of a preference gene for maintaining features like the eye pattern would be entirely consistent with a wise Creator.

5.11 Problems with the theory of sexual selection

The idea that the peacock tail could evolve by a long series of genetic mistakes is absurd. Even if future studies do reveal preference genes in the peahen for aesthetic features, there are still immense problems with the theory of sexual selection. This section describes six problems:

I WHY SHOULD THE FEMALE SELECT A 'BEAUTIFUL' FEATURE?

Sexual selection is based on a particular fashion which is generally determined by the preference genes of the female.[18] According to the theory of sexual selection, the fashion could be for long tails, bright colours or certain patterns. However, there is no reason why a fashion should always be a 'beautiful' fashion. According to evolution, preference genes appear by totally random processes and so they could involve a preference for ugly as well as beautiful features. In reality, however, male creatures like the peacock do not have a mixture of beautiful and ugly features but an overwhelming presence of beautiful features. This conclusion is not a subjective one but is based on objective observations such as the presence of precise patterns like the eye of the peacock. Indeed, evolutionists fully agree that the decorative features of creatures like the peacock are entirely beautiful.

To overcome the problem that females always prefer 'beautiful' features, evolutionists have invented the 'good genes' theory which proposes that beauty is directly related to health and fitness.[19] However, whilst a human being might associate beauty with fitness, there is no reason why a bird should make such a value judgement. Also, the decorative features found in nature are so overwhelmingly beautiful that there would need to be an extremely strong correlation between beauty and health to explain the existence of such overwhelming beauty, and there is no evidence for such a strong correlation. The 'good genes' theory is an interesting example of a desperate quick-fix solution where the theory of evolution does not work!

II HOW CAN THE SEXUAL SELECTION CYCLE START BY CHANCE?

Another big problem with the theory of sexual selection is the question of how the sexual selection cycle can start by chance. The cycle cannot start until there is both a preference gene in the female *and* a trait gene in the male. Therefore, for a sexual selection cycle to get started there must be the appearance of at least two new genes in the DNA. Since genes contain complex information and since the preference gene and trait gene are useless on their own, it must be concluded that sexual selection could never evolve in small steps.

To overcome the problem of the need for the simultaneous appearance of two new genes, evolutionists have proposed that the two genes appear at different times in the following way.[20] First, a female spontaneously produces a preference gene for a male with, say, a long tail. This gene lies dormant for perhaps many generations without any opportunity to be exercised. Then one day, a male spontaneously gains a gene which produces a long tail. The female then selects that male and the resulting offspring have both the trait gene and the preference gene. These offspring not only contain a long tail in the males but a preference for the long tail in the females. Therefore, the sexual selection cycle is in place and ready to develop long tails.

At first, the scenario of two new genes arising independently at different times may seem plausible. However, this explanation is misleading because it does not mention that there must be a chance meeting between the right female and the right male. A female peacock may only bump into a handful of males in her lifetime and this may be a tiny fraction of the whole population. There is no use a male having a particular beautiful trait unless he is in the right place at the right time to meet the right female who happens to prefer that trait. Also, whereas it could be argued that a female preference could lie dormant for a long period, it cannot be argued that a male trait could lie dormant because the male trait would always be visible and would be a disadvantage in terms of escaping from predators.

The starting of one sexual selection cycle is very difficult to explain by chance. However, when a creature contains many separate aesthetic features, the problem becomes even more pronounced because many cycles must be started. In the case of the peacock, there are many aesthetic features in the tail. In addition, the peacock also has several aesthetic features in the rest of its body. For example, it has a bright blue neck, patterns around the eye, a crown on the head and speckled contour feathers. This array of features would require not one set of preference and trait genes but many sets of preference and trait genes.

III HOW CAN THE FEMALE APPRECIATE SUBTLE FEATURES?

It may well be possible that a peahen has a preference for prominent features such as a long tail or bright colours. However, there are some extremely subtle features in the peacock which are not easy to recognise. These subtle features include the absence of a stem in the upper part of the eye pattern, the brown colouring of the stem near to the eye pattern and the intricate shape of the T feathers. It may be reasonable to argue that a peahen could recognise whether a peacock had lost its eye feathers or T feathers. However, to discern subtle changes in these feathers would require tremendous detailed observation. Features such as the narrow stem and the local brown colouring are so subtle that many people do not notice them. In addition, it is necessary to get quite close to the feather to recognise such features. Since peahens do not make close visual inspections of peacocks, they would need incredibly powerful vision in order to observe the subtle features. However, there is no evidence that peahens possess such vision.

IV SOME FEATURES CONTAIN IRREDUCIBLE MECHANISMS

Another major problem for the theory of sexual selection is that some of the structures that produce the aesthetic features in the peacock tail are irreducible. One example of an irreducible structure is the thin-film interference. The production of thin-film interference in a feather simultaneously requires at least a flat barbule structure, one keratin layer and the correct thickness of the keratin layer. Since evolution is supposed to work by changing one characteristic at a time, evolution cannot explain how thin-film interference could evolve. For example, if there was a random gene mutation that suddenly caused a barbule to become flat, this change would not be enough to cause thin-film interference. Even if a barbule were to become flat and acquire a layer of keratin, this would still not produce a thin-film colour unless the keratin was the right thickness. The only way to produce iridescent feathers is to make a fully functioning flat thin film from the beginning.

V SOME FEATURES CONTAIN IRREDUCIBLE BEAUTY

According to evolution, a complex pattern like the eye pattern in the peacock tail feathers has evolved by the accumulation of hundreds of genetic mistakes occurring over vast periods of time. However, patterns like the blue ellipsoid in the eye are irreducible (i.e. they require several features to be simultaneously present in order for there to be a pattern with aesthetic merit). If only one patch of blue colour was to randomly appear on the peacock tail, this would not produce a pattern with aesthetic merit. Such a random change would arguably cause the peahen to deselect, not select the pattern. Therefore, the blue colour would not survive long enough to evolve into an ellipsoid. Since evolution requires every step change to have a selective advantage, it is very difficult for evolution to explain how the eye pattern could evolve.

VI FIELD STUDIES HAVE SHOWN DEGENERATION OF BEAUTY

In 2001 there was a publication of some field studies which showed that beautiful features were generally being lost and not gained. The paper was entitled: 'Widespread loss of sexually selected traits: how the peacock lost its spots'. The paper says the following:

> …recent phylogenic studies have revealed a surprising trend. In many different groups of organisms, the male trait appears to have been lost in some species. This trend is surprising for several reasons. First the pattern was largely (but not entirely) unknown until very recently. For example, Andersson's thorough review of the field of sexual selection does not discuss the loss of male traits. Second, this pattern seems to be extremely widespread.[21]

The widespread loss of male traits is a major blow to the theory of sexual selection. The loss of beauty is exactly what would be expected from gene mutations. Gene mutations cause random errors to occur in the genetic code. Therefore, gene mutations can only cause a loss of information and not a gain in information. In addition, mutations can only distort mechanisms and not create them. The fact that beautiful features are being lost and not gained is tremendous evidence against the theory of evolution. Creationists are not surprised by the loss of beauty because this is consistent with the effects of the Fall.

5.12 Admissions by evolutionists

There are some remarkable admissions by evolutionists about the wonder of the design of bird feathers and about the weakness of the theory of sexual selection. These admissions confirm that bird coloration provides tremendous evidence for design.

Mason says the following about thin-film interference:

The theory of thin films as the cause of iridescence, although it fits all the observed facts, cannot but inspire one to marvel at the perfection of nature's method of producing these colours with such uniformity through successive generations, especially when a slight general variation in thickness of the films of the feathers of a bird, such as a peacock, would be enough to alter its coloration completely.[22]

This is an important quote because Mason's studies on the colour of peacock feathers are referred to by most modern texts on bird coloration. Notice how the author refers to the 'perfection of nature's method'. Also notice how the author marvels at how the thin film is maintained in successive generations. If it is hard to understand how the peacock 'maintains' its delicate structures through successive generations, then how does the evolutionist explain how it could have evolved from ordinary tail feathers?

Some evolutionists recognise that the presence of beauty presents a particularly difficult problem for the theory of evolution. For example, Darwin himself recognised that subtle aesthetic features in birds like the details of the peacock tail are very difficult to explain by evolution. Darwin said:

Many will declare that it is utterly incredible that a female bird should be able to appreciate fine shading and exquisite patterns. It is undoubtedly a marvellous fact that she should possess this almost human degree of taste.[23]

The peacock tail was one of the things in nature which seemed to give Charles Darwin doubts about the validity of his theory of evolution. Darwin once said:

The sight of a feather in a peacock's tail, whenever I gaze at it, makes me feel sick![24]

Helen Cronin, a leading modern-day writer on sexual selection, has acknowledged the basic contradiction between survival of the fittest and sexual selection:

With our other eponymous hero, the peacock, the difficulty lies in his splendid tail. It flies in the face of natural selection. Far from being efficient, utilitarian and beneficial, it is flamboyant, ornamental and a burden to its bearer. And peacock tails—ornaments, colours, songs, dances—abound throughout the animal kingdom, from insects to fish to mammals.[25]

One of the leading A-level biology books in the United Kingdom teaches students that sexual selection is a contentious issue:

This process is called sexual selection. Its importance was first recognised by Darwin, though it has been a contentious issue ever since.[26]

John Maynard Smith has made this very significant admission about the difficulty of the theory of sexual selection:

No topic [beauty] in evolutionary biology has presented more difficulties for theorists.[27]

I personally agree with this last statement. The presence of added beauty in the world presents an immense problem for evolution. Only intelligent design can explain the existence of beauty for beauty's sake.

5.13 Beautiful colours in birds

The peacock is only one of many birds which have beautiful colouring. The feathers of birds contain a virtually complete range of colours from pure white through yellow, red, green and blue to black. This is remarkable because, like other animals, the only pigment in birds is melanin and this produces only shades of brown and black. The existence of colours in feathers requires very complex physical processes to take place.

There are three main ways that colour is produced in feathers. Some colours are produced by pigments, which may be melanin or additional pigments obtained from plants. Some colours are produced by special optical effects such as the scattering of light or thin-film interference. Some colours are produced by a combination of pigments and optical effects. Table 5–1 shows a range of colours found in birds with examples of the physical processes that produce the colours.

Table 5–1 Examples of bird colouring

COLOUR	BIRD	PHYSICAL PROCESS
White	Swan	Reflection and refraction of white light
Yellow	Canary	Carotenoid pigment
Pink	Flamingo	Carotenoid pigment
Red	Touracos	Porphyrins pigment
Green	Parrot	Combination of carotenoid pigment and scattering
Blue	Budgerigar	Scattering of light
Brown	Thrush	Melanin pigment
Black	Crow	Melanin pigment
Iridescent colours	Peacock	Interference of light

White is produced when a transparent feather has an internal structure which reflects and refracts all wavelengths of white light. The colour blue is produced when light is scattered by tiny air-filled cavities in a transparent keratin material.[28] The scattering of light produces blue because scattering intensity is much greater for light of a higher frequency and blue has the highest frequency of the visible colour range. The colour blue can also be produced by thin-film interference.

Many of the world's most beautiful birds, such as birds of paradise, live in tropical regions. However, there are some very beautiful birds in temperate regions such as Europe. Beautifully-coloured birds in Europe include the kingfisher, waxwing and blue tit. Even some ordinary birds contain some very beautiful details. For example, the town pigeon has a beautiful iridescent collar and the jay contains a patch of beautiful blue barred feathers on its body. The outstanding beauty of birds provides great evidence of design.

5.14 The effect of the Fall

It is certain that the world was more beautiful before the Fall because God called the creation 'very good' at the end of the creation week (Genesis 1:31). One of the reasons why the world became less beautiful after the Fall was almost certainly the introduction of the predator-prey relationship. The sudden existence of the predator-prey relationship meant that the vast majority of creatures needed camouflage to survive. The need for camouflage would have put a very severe restriction on the amount of coloration and patterns that was possible in creatures after the Fall. For example, the vast majority of land animals are very vulnerable to predators and so must have a relatively dull coloration in order to blend in with the surroundings.

The distribution of colours in creatures around the world strongly supports the idea that the predator-prey relationship has had a major effect on beauty. For example, in dense rain forests, many birds are relatively protected from predators because of their flying abilities and because of the sheltered environment. In such cases, it is interesting that many of the birds are coloured very beautifully. It is as if these birds have kept much of the beauty they had before the Fall because there was no reason for them to be camouflaged after the Fall. It is interesting to note that birds of paradise are so named because they have such spectacular beauty it is as if they have not changed since being in the original 'paradise'. Since birds of paradise live in dense forests, it may well be true that they were not changed much at the time of the Fall.

The kingfisher is also an example that supports the predator-prey theory. Most predators need to be camouflaged in order to be inconspicuous to their prey as they approach them. The white polar bear and golden lion are two examples of well-camouflaged predators. However, the kingfisher is an exception to this rule because it flies so fast and dives so quickly into the water that its colour makes little difference to its level of concealment. Since the colouring of the kingfisher does not reduce its success as a predator, it is able to have very bright and beautiful colouring.

Another effect of the Fall is that some of the beautiful features found in nature are gradually being lost. As mentioned earlier, there is actual observational evidence that this is currently happening. Therefore, early generations of people would have seen a greater degree of beauty in creatures than we do now. Thankfully, there is still immense beauty in the world today.

5.15 The goodness and wisdom of God in creation

The beauty of the peacock tail is so great that it is no wonder that it made Charles Darwin feel sick. In contrast, when Christians look at the tail of the peacock, they can feel a wonderful assurance that there is a Creator who is infinite in wisdom and that He has been very good to mankind in putting such beauty into the world. The Bible clearly teaches that God deliberately put beauty into the world. For example, in Genesis we read that 'God made every tree grow that is pleasant to the sight' (Genesis 2:9). Also in Job we read that 'By His spirit He adorned the heavens' (Job 26:13). These examples show that beauty is no accident but the result of the conscious provision of a loving heavenly Father. Not only has God put great beauty into the world, but He has also given the human being a brain which has the capacity for appreciating beauty. When we observe beauty in this world we should remember that the Creator of the world is more beautiful than the most beautiful parts of creation. Even now we can appreciate the beauty of the Lord (Psalm 27:4).

Notes on Chapter 5

1   A paper on the peacock tail, based on the contents of this chapter, has been published in the AIG Technical Journal in a paper entitled: 'The beauty of the peacock tail and the problems with the theory of sexual selection', *TJ* 15(2), pp. 94–102, 2001.

2   **Pye, D.**, *The nature and aesthetics of design*, Barrie and Jenkins, London, 1978.

3   Quoted from: **Cronin, H.**, *The ant and the peacock*, Cambridge University Press, Cambridge, Great Britain, p. 183, 1991.

4   Some of the peacock display feathers have a few centimetres of fluffy barbs at their root to perform the function of thermal insulation. However, the fluffy barbs are such a minor detail that the description of 'display feather' is generally used by biologists.

5   **King, A.S. and McLelland, J.**, *Birds—their structure and form*, Bailliere Tindall, p. 15, 1984.

6   **Sager, E.**, 'Morphologishce Analyse der Musterbildung beim Pfauenrad', *Revue Suisse de Zoologie, Geneve* **62**(2):116, 1955.

7   **Mason, C.W.**, 'Structural colours in feathers II', *Journal of Physical Chemistry* **27**:440, 1923.

8   **Mason, C.W.**, *op. cit.*, p. 416.

9   **Mason, C.W.**, *op. cit.*, p. 417.

10 **Mason, C.W.**, *op. cit.*, p. 416.

11 **Mason, C.W.,** *op. cit.,* p. 443.

12 **Mason, C.W.,** *op. cit.,* p. 442.

13 **Marshall, A.J. (Ed.),** *Biology and comparative physiology of birds,* Academic Press, London, p. 225, 1960.

14 **Voitkevich, A.A.,** *The feathers and plumage of birds,* London: Sidgewick and Jackson, p. 34, 1966.

15 **Darwin, C.,** *The Descent of Man,* John Murray, London, p. 412, 1871.

16 **Cronin, H.,** *The ant and the peacock,* Cambridge University Press, Cambridge, Great Britain, p. 118, 1991.

17 **Darwin, C.,** *The Descent of Man,* John Murray, London, p. 349, 1888.

18 **Cronin, H.,** *op. cit.,* p. 202.

19 **Cronin, H.,** *op. cit.,* p. 186.

20 www.talkorigins.org/faqs/faq-intro-to-biology.html, p. 7, 2001

21 **Wiens, J.J.,** 'Widespread loss of sexually selected traits: how the peacock lost its spots', *Trends in Ecology & Evolution,* Vol. 16, No.9, September 2001.

22 **Mason, C.W.,** *op. cit.* p. 444.

23 **Darwin, C.,** *The Descent of Man,* John Murray, London, p. 412, 1871.

24 **Darwin, F.,** (Ed), *The life and Letters of Charles Darwin,* John Murray, London, Vol. 2, p. 296, 1887.

25 **Cronin, H.,** *op. cit.,* p. 3.

26 **Roberts, M.B.V.,** *Biology a functional approach,* 4th Ed, Nelson, p. 613.

27 **Maynard Smith, J.,** 'Theories of Sexual Selection', *TREE,* 6: 146–151, 1991.

28 **King, A.S. and McLelland, J.,** *op. cit.* p. 39.

Added beauty in bird song

Let everything that has breath praise the Lord (Psalm 150:6).

Apart from the human voice, birds produce some of the purest and most beautiful sounds known to man. Bird song has inspired some of the greatest classical music composers and writers. More recently, scientists have been astounded by the singing abilities of songbirds. This chapter defines beauty in music and shows why bird song contains amazing evidence of design.

6.1 Beauty in music

David would take a harp and play it with his hand. Then Saul would become refreshed and well (1 Samuel 16:23).

In the latter part of his reign, King Saul sometimes became distressed in his spirit. One of the ways in which Saul was made to feel better was through the hearing of music played on the harp.

Beauty in music can be produced by attributes such as melody, rhythm, harmony, variety and unity or any combination of such attributes. Melody is produced by a series of agreeable and varied notes; rhythm is produced by a pattern of regular beats; harmony is produced by a combination of notes; variety is produced by changes in pattern; and unity is produced by having a consistent theme throughout a piece of music. These attributes are very real attributes. Therefore, even though the beauty of a piece of music cannot be quantified, and even though the perception of beauty is partly an emotional response, beauty in music is a very real thing. In fact, modern research has shown that the human brain has specific areas dedicated to appreciating music.

Beauty in music is an important evidence of intelligent design because beautiful music cannot be produced by accident. Attributes such as melody, rhythm and harmony require skilful and creative planning by an intelligent source. The fact that musicians and composers must study for many years, learning about the technical aspects of music, shows that beautiful music cannot just appear by chance.

6.2 Songbirds

Of the 9,000 or so species of bird alive today, about 5,000 are passerines (mainly tree-perching) and about 4,000 are non-passerines (mainly non tree-perching). Of the 5,000 passerines, about 4,000 are songbirds (oscines). Many of the most musical songbirds, like the nightingale, blackbird, song thrush and robin, live in temperate regions such as Europe and North America. An interesting feature of birds is that they usually do not possess very beautiful feathers *and* a beautiful voice. For example, the nightingale and blackbird produce very beautiful songs but have a relatively ordinary appearance. In contrast, parrots and peacocks are very beautifully coloured but cannot produce beautiful songs.

Songbirds make two types of sound: calls and songs. Calls are short and simple sounds that have the purpose of communicating a simple message, such as a warning signal or distress signal. In contrast, songs are long and complicated and can have a great deal of musical content. At first, it may appear as though songbirds produce random notes. However, careful listening to songbirds reveals that their songs are not random at all. For example, if a particular songbird is studied over several days, it will be found that the same song is repeated with great accuracy on different occasions. Also, birds are able to copy the songs of other birds, showing that birds are able to hear, learn and repeat music in a deliberate way.

In most cases it is the male bird that sings, although there are species where both males and females sing. There are particular times of day when singing is most common, such as the morning 'dawn chorus'. Song is known to perform at least three communication roles in songbirds. The most common role is that of *territorial defence* which takes place throughout the year. A male bird advertises its ownership of a territory by singing in that territory. Another common role of bird song is that of *courtship* during the breeding season. In general, it is the male bird which attracts the female by song. Another role of bird song, which is quite common in tropical areas with dense vegetation, is that of *recognition* between a pair of courting birds. Dense vegetation makes it difficult for birds to locate their partner by sight and so they use song as an aid to recognition and bonding. In such cases, both the male and female sing and it is also common for them to perform duets.

6.3 The beauty of bird song

Since birds visit gardens, most people have a general awareness of the beauty of bird song. However, not many people have listened closely to bird song and appreciated the fine aspects of musical beauty. A close study of bird song reveals that birds are extremely skilful musicians. In fact, in the last few decades, much research has been carried out into bird song and this has revealed an astonishing degree of sophistication and musical content. Bird song is so intricate that it sometimes requires a degree qualification in music to fully appreciate all that birds can do.

A typical bird song lasts between four and twenty seconds and contains a series of distinct musical phrases, each of which consists of several notes. Even though most songs last less than twenty seconds, they often contain many phrases and a large number of notes. For example, a chaffinch can sing up to 45 notes per second[1] and there can be several hundred notes per song.

A short excerpt from the song of the wood pewee is shown in Fig. 6–1.[2] This section of song consists of four phrases and contains musical

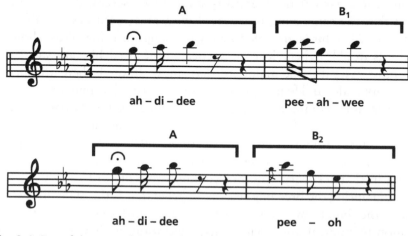

Fig. 6–1 Part of the song of the wood pewee

attributes of melody, rhythm, variety and unity. An important thing to notice in this example is that there are different sections in the song that are closely related. Of the four phrases shown, the first phrase is repeated almost exactly in the third section and the other two phrases represent an appropriate and pleasant variation on the theme. This unity and variety is remarkable because human composers must exercise creativity and careful planning to produce such effects.

Music composed by man contains more consonant intervals than dissonant intervals in order to produce pleasant-sounding melody and harmony. (An interval is produced when two notes are played consecutively or simultaneously). Consonant intervals are generally pleasant-sounding and they include the minor 3rd, major 3rd, perfect 4th, perfect 5th, minor 6th, major 6th and octave. Dissonant intervals are generally not pleasant-sounding and they include the minor 2nd, major 2nd, augmented 4th, minor 7th and major 7th. If songbirds produced just random intervals in their songs, then there should be an equal number of all types of intervals in bird song. However, studies of various songbirds have shown that bird song clearly contains many more consonant intervals than dissonant intervals.[3] This means that there are objective reasons for classifying bird song as music with a high degree of aesthetic merit.

6.4 The bird voice: a masterpiece of design

Even though songbirds are very small, they are able to produce a powerful sound that can carry for long distances. The sound-producing organ of the bird is called the syrinx. It is the equivalent of the human voice box or larynx. Like the larynx, the syrinx contains delicate membranes which vibrate and generate soundwaves when air from the lungs passes over them. There are some special features in songbirds which enable them to produce beautiful songs:

I SPECIAL DOUBLE VOICE

Songbirds have the special ability to produce sounds independently from two voices. Whereas humans have one set of vibrating membranes in the larynx, birds have two sets of membranes in the syrinx. The human larynx is located at the top of the trachea (the tube between the two bronchi and the throat) and so receives air from both lungs. In contrast, the bird membranes are located at the top of each bronchus (the two tubes between the lungs and the trachea) and so each set of membranes receives air from each lung independently. Amazingly, each of these voice mechanisms has independent nerve connections with the brain so that the bird can simultaneously produce different sounds from each voice.[4] The sounds from the two voices may be produced at the same time or at different times. Close monitoring of bird song has demonstrated that some birds can produce two notes at the same time. Double notes have been identified in the brown thrasher, gouldian finch and reed warbler. The blue jay has been reported to be able to sing the notes of a major chord simultaneously. After sounds are produced from the two voice mechanisms, the sounds are fed into the trachea together and then travel onto the higher vocal tract (the throat and mouth). One of the ways in which birds vary sound is to stretch the vocal tract and to vary the amount of opening of the beak.

II SPECIAL CONNECTIONS IN THE BRAIN

The production of bird song requires sophisticated control from the brain, especially since a song may contain up to several dozen notes per second. A bird has the additional challenge of co-ordinating the notes from the two separate voice mechanisms. Neurobiologists have discovered that there is a complex brain pathway which controls the production of songs.[5] There is also another pathway which is involved with the learning of songs and this is connected to the pathway for controlling the production of songs. It is amazing to think that when a songbird is singing, it is not producing random notes but actually a song that is written in the brain of the bird!

III SPECIAL METHOD OF BREATHING

Human singers know that one of the challenges of singing is to be able to take periodic breaths without disrupting the flow of music. However, birds have an incredible ability to sing for quite long periods without appearing to take any breath. Recent studies have provided evidence that songbirds are able to take mini-breaths that are so short that they do not produce any discernable gaps in the song. For example, there is evidence that canaries take mini-breaths after singing each syllable at a rate of up to 27 notes per second.[6]

There is also evidence that when canaries sing, they produce most of the sounds from their left lung whilst the right lung is used mainly for breathing.

6.5 Advanced musical features

Some songbirds have a particularly high degree of musical skill in terms of repertoire or complexity of song. This section describes some of the most remarkable abilities of songbirds.

I GREAT REPERTOIRES

A repertoire is the number of songs that a type of bird is able to remember and reproduce. Five of the largest song repertoires recorded by bird experts are shown below:[7]

BIRD	SIZE OF REPERTOIRE
European blackbird	22–48
Mockingbird	53–150
Marsh wren	33–162
Song thrush	138–219
Nightingale	100–300

These birds must have a fantastic amount of information in their brains to recall and reproduce such a large number of separate songs. The list helps to explain why the nightingale is famous for its great variety of songs. Amazingly, scientists have found that the nightingale usually goes through its repertoire without repeating the same song for quite some time. Studies have found that the nightingale will only repeat a particular song after intervals of typically 70 songs.[8] Therefore, you would typically need to listen to a nightingale sing 70 songs before hearing the same song again. And when you do hear the same song again, it is invariably sung with perfect accuracy!

II MIMICKING

Birds often copy the songs of other birds within the same species. However, some birds, like the marsh warbler, have the ability to copy the songs of other species of bird. Some birds are even able to copy man-made sounds. In May 2001 there was a report of a passenger on a railway platform thinking that their mobile phone was ringing, only to find that the ringing was produced by a nearby bird![9]

III TRANSPOSITIONS

One of the most astounding musical abilities of birds is their control of the key in which a song is sung. Many birds have what is musically known as 'absolute pitch', which is the ability to determine exactly what key they sing in without reference to any other sounds. If you hear a bird singing a song in G major on a particular day, then you will often find that the bird will still be singing the song in G major on subsequent occasions. Absolute pitch is such a sophisticated skill that very few human singers have it even after training. There is also evidence that birds deliberately transpose songs from one key to another![10]

IV MATCHED COUNTERSINGING

When two male birds are in hearing range in neighbouring territories, they will often take it in turns to sing to each other. Each bird will typically sing for several seconds and then stop to allow the neighbouring bird to reply with a song. Having heard the first song, the neighbour will then sing his own song for several seconds and then wait for a reply. These exchanges of songs may go on for several minutes. A common feature of such song exchanges is that the birds will deliberately sing a song which compliments the song of the neighbour. It may be that the birds choose to sing a song from their repertoire that is complimentary to the neighbour's song. However, it may also be that they spontaneously compose a 'variation on a theme', where the theme is provided by the neighbour's song. Such singing is called matched countersinging because each song matches the other. Matched countersinging can be commonly observed in male blackbirds in the summer. It is interesting to note that some of the most beautiful music in operas involves matched countersinging between two singers. Such countersinging in man-made music requires great planning and design. In a similar way, the matched countersinging in birds provides remarkable evidence of design!

V DUETTING

Duets involve two birds combining their voices to produce one song. The two members of the duet are usually a pair of courting birds. One example of a duet occurs with a courting pair of tawny owls when they produce their characteristic 'to-whit-oo-oo' song. The 'to-whit' is produced by the

Key: X = 1st bird, Y = 2nd bird

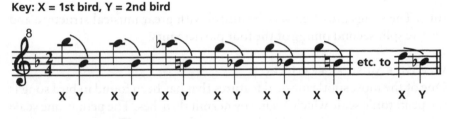

Fig. 6–2 Recorded duet of the African shrike

female whilst the male produces the 'oo-oo' to finish the phrase. Some pairs of songbirds, such as the African shrike, African robin chat and Eastern whipbird, perform what is called antiphonal singing where two birds sing alternate notes in a song. Antiphonal singing requires knowledge of the duet by both partners and split second timing in the execution of the duet. In some forms of man-made music, like operas, trained singers perform antiphonal singing. This is considered to be very skilful and impressive and yet birds can already do this. Bird duets give great evidence of design! An example of a recorded duet by the African shrike is shown in Fig. 6–2.

VI MATCHED DUETTING

Studies of African shrikes have shown that these birds sometimes perform matched duetting in a group of four. An example of a recorded matched duet[11] by the African shrike is shown in Fig. 6–3. The quartet is usually made of two pairs of courting birds. In a typical quartet, there will be one pair of courting shrikes singing in one territory and a second pair of courting shrikes singing in an adjacent territory. The two pairs of courting birds will deliberately compose a song with four parts over a period of

Key: X = 1st bird, Y = 2nd bird, U = 3rd bird, V = 4th bird

Fig. 6–3 Recorded quartet of the African shrike

time. The songs are often very beautiful with great musical structure and involve split second timing of the four participants!

VII OTHER MUSICAL FEATURES

One of the most subtle musical features that has been found in bird song is the pentatonic scale which is sung by hermit thrushes. The pentatonic scale is the scale produced by the black notes on the piano. (The pentatonic scale can also be produced by other notes if they have the same intervals as the black notes.) The pentatonic scale is used in traditional Asian music and is also sometimes used by western composers. The right-hand part in Chopin's Etude in G flat major consists almost entirely of black notes. Another feature of some bird song is the presence of a flourishing end-phrase. The end-phrase of the chaffinch has been shown to consist of a flourish with longer notes.[12] This provides remarkable evidence of design because in human composition it is common practice to finish a piece with longer notes and a concluding phrase in order to show the listener that the music has come to a conclusion.

6.6 The purpose of bird song

The beauty of bird song is so great that it must be concluded that the most important purpose of bird song is to bring pleasure to the Creator and to man. This conclusion is totally rejected by evolutionists. The evolutionist argues that since bird song has communication roles such as territorial defence, courtship and recognition, this must mean that bird song has not been created for the pleasure of man. However, the fact that song performs communication roles for birds does *not* automatically mean that bird song exists only for the sake of birds. The complexity of bird song is so much greater than is required for communication that communication cannot be the only purpose of bird song. There are actually two very logical reasons why the Creator would give bird song communication roles such as territorial defence, courtship and recognition.

I TRIGGER FOR SONG

By giving birds a need to sing all through the year, this ensures that birds sing often for the enjoyment of man. If birds did not have to sing to communicate messages, then they might not sing at all. Therefore, the use of song in territorial defence, courtship and recognition is a clever way of ensuring that the beauty of bird song can be appreciated by man.

II CONSERVATION OF BEAUTY

Another advantage of song having communication roles is that it helps to conserve the beauty of bird song. If singing were not needed for any communication role, then it would be more likely that song could disappear due to gene mutations. For example, if a bird of a particular species stopped singing due to gene mutations, and there was no communication role for its singing, it could find itself at an advantage because it would be less conspicuous and would use less energy. This is an example of where 'loss' of information in the genetic code can be an advantage. However, since singing does have communication roles in birds, it is not an advantage for a bird to stop singing.

Territorial singing, courtship singing and singing for recognition are so useful for triggering songs and conserving beauty that these communication roles actually add weight to the argument that bird song has been created for the pleasure of man. The evolutionary idea that bird song has not been made for the pleasure of man is totally without justification.

6.7 Problems with the theory of evolution of territorial song

Many people assume that the theory of evolution proposes that bird song evolved mainly due to sexual selection. However, this assumption is wrong. Leading evolutionists believe that bird song evolved mainly for territorial purposes. Two leading experts in bird song have recently stated:

White suggested that male rivalry for space was the most important function of bird song. With the publication of Eliot Howard's influential book on territory, the concept became widely known, and ever since then the view that bird song developed primarily as a territorial proclamation to rival males has held sway. In his major review, Armstrong clearly regarded 'territorial song' as the most important type of song produced by male birds.[13]

The reason why territorial defence is considered to have been the driving force behind the supposed evolution of bird song is that territorial singing is the most common singing carried out by male birds. Whilst male birds use song to attract females in the breeding season, territorial song is used throughout the year.

Evolutionists argue that singing gives male birds a survival advantage because it helps them to avoid fights with other males of the same species and thus be better placed to produce offspring. Catchpole and Slater say this about the advantage of territorial song:

It seems that by singing, territorial males may have a number of advantages, such as reducing their chances of injury in fights. Instead of constantly chasing and fighting off rivals, they are able to conserve valuable energy and resources, which can then be used to enhance future reproductive success.[14]

However, just because song is used to advertise presence in a territory, this does not mean that song is the only way of advertising presence or that song must have evolved by genetic mistakes. The theory that bird song evolved for territorial defence has immense problems. Some of these problems are explained as follows:

1 WHY SHOULD SONGS BE BEAUTIFUL?

If bird song evolved simply to advertise the presence of a male in a territory then one would expect songs to be very simple. The fact that songbirds make simple calls to communicate other messages, such as distress calls, shows that bird sounds do not need to be complicated in order to communicate a message. Also, the fact that many other animals use crude shouts and roars to protect their territory shows that territorial defence needs only simple communication. Despite the simple needs of territorial defence, bird song is often extremely complicated and contains very subtle musical beauty.

According to evolution, there was a time when birds used just simple calls to advertise their presence. Then, following genetic mistakes, the calls gradually turned into beautiful songs. According to evolution, each time a beautiful feature was added to the song (by gene mutation), other males found this increase in beauty more intimidating and so beautiful songs gave survival advantages. However, there is no reason why beautiful songs should be more frightening than simple calls. Why should a rival male find a bird sound more frightening when it contains musical attributes of melody, rhythm, harmony or variety? Why should a rival male find the pentatonic scale or a major chord more frightening than a simple call? Also, if beautiful song is more intimidating than simple calls, then why do not all animals sing to defend their territory?! Evolution has no explanation as to why there should be selective pressures for 'beautiful' songs.

II WHY SHOULD MALES COPY EACH OTHER?
Matched countersinging presents a particularly big problem for evolution because many male birds seem to enjoy singing with neighbouring male birds! Catchpole and Slater say this about matched countersinging:

Another form of coordinated singing is the matching that often occurs between territorial neighbours. It is striking that, when two such males sing against each other, they will often sing the same song type if both have it in their repertoires. Armstrong suggested that this was 'naming an opponent in song duels'...Bertram wrote of matched countersinging as involving 'flinging an insult back at the rival'. It may be, as this suggests, that hearing a song closely matching its own is a particularly effective deterrent for neighbours or other intruders.[15]

This quotation illustrates the absurdity of evolutionary thinking. When two male birds take it in turns to sing to each other with matching songs, this produces a musical effect of the most profound beauty. The evolutionary idea that the beauty of matched countersinging is simply there because the birds want to 'fling insults at each other' is absurd! If two male birds are singing insults to each other then why should each bird patiently wait for the other to finish his song before replying? When two people are having an argument, it is usually the case that the participants interrupt and contradict each other. However, such behaviour is not seen in bird song. Matched countersinging provides wonderful evidence that bird song has been created for the sake of man.

III THE DAWN CHORUS
Another problem for the theory of evolution is the presence of the dawn

chorus. The evolutionist rejects the idea that the Creator has planned the dawn chorus for the pleasure of man. Having rejected man-centred purpose, the evolutionist has to try and invent naturalistic reasons for the existence of the dawn chorus. One idea that has been proposed is that sound travels better at dawn and so singing is more effective at this time. Another idea is that feeding conditions are relatively poor in the morning and so there is more time to sing. Whilst these ideas may have an element of truth, they cannot explain why there is such a forceful crescendo of song. In fact, there is such a volume of singing at dawn that it is difficult to see any benefit of singing from the point of view of a bird. When every male bird is perched and singing simultaneously, it is very difficult for an individual male bird to hear himself let alone get a message across to anyone else!

IV IRREDUCIBLE MECHANISMS

Evolution has no explanation as to how the voice mechanisms of birds could have evolved. In fact, the voice mechanism could not have evolved step by step because many parts are needed to be in place simultaneously for the mechanism to work. For example, there is no point in having two voice mechanisms if they are not independently connected to the brain or if the information for producing sophisticated songs does not exist in the brain. To propose that the double voice of a songbird could have evolved by a series of genetic mistakes is a most amazing claim. And to propose that the voice of a bird evolved just to advertise its presence to rival males is simply absurd.

6.8 Problems with the theory of sexual selection

The fact that some birds sing mainly in the breeding season is used as evidence that sexual selection has played a significant role in the supposed evolution of at least some bird song. However, even though song is used to attract females, this does not mean that song is the only thing that can attract females or that song must have evolved by genetic mistakes. The theory that a process of sexual selection could 'evolve' beautiful songs by a long series of genetic mistakes has immense problems. Some of these problems are explained as follows:

I HOW COULD THE SEXUAL SELECTION CYCLE GET STARTED?
As with the peacock tail feathers, there is no explanation as to how a sexual selection cycle for bird song could start by a single chance accident. The theory of sexual selection requires that the female evolves a *preference* gene for a beautiful feature and that the male evolves a *trait* gene for the same beautiful feature. Since evolution requires that every single genetic mistake must give a selective advantage, it is not possible for the supposed sexual selection cycle to start by chance.

II WHY SHOULD A FEMALE CHOOSE A BEAUTIFUL SONG?
There is no explanation as to why the female should choose a 'beautiful' song rather than just random notes. Since preference and trait genes are supposed to appear by random accidents, there should be at least as much ugly singing as beautiful singing by songbirds. However, bird experts agree that songbirds produce overwhelmingly beautiful songs.

6.9 Problems with the theory of evolution of song for recognition

In areas where there is dense vegetation and visibility is limited, some birds like the African shrike use song as an aid to recognising their partner and forming a bond with them. However, even though bird song is used for recognition and bonding, this does not mean that beautiful songs are the only things that enable recognition or that song must have evolved by genetic mistakes.

I WHY SHOULD BIRDS SING DUETS?
To sing a duet requires two birds to be able to compose a song in complete co-operation. As well as composing the song, the two birds must agree who is going to perform which part. Having learnt the duet, the birds must then have the musical ability to recall and sing the duet in tune. The ability of some birds to sing duets has astonished scientists who believe in evolution. Catchpole and Slater say this about duet singing:

Some duets have phenomenal precision of timing. Indeed, while bouts may overlap, the sounds themselves may not do so, the birds fitting their sounds together so precisely that it is hard to believe that more than one individual is involved. This form of duetting, in which male and female use different notes and sing alternately, is known as antiphonal singing…A good example of it is in the African robin chat, in which a series of elements from the two birds alternate, with very little overlap between them yet astonishingly brief latencies.[16]

If it is hard to believe that two birds can have the skill to perform precise antiphonal singing, then surely it is harder to believe that singing has evolved in birds by genetic mistakes! Not surprisingly, it is difficult to find an evolutionist who is brave enough (or mad enough) to attempt to describe how duetting could evolve by genetic mistakes. How can anyone explain how two birds could ever obtain the skill of developing duets with a partner by an accumulation of chance genetic mistakes?

II WHY SHOULD BIRDS SING MATCHED DUETS?

The idea that a bird could acquire the ability to sing duets with a partner by genetic mistakes is an incredible idea. However, to propose that two pairs of duetting birds should develop the skill to sing in a quartet by genetic mistakes is absolutely absurd. Evolutionists have proposed that two pairs of birds sing in a quartet as part of territorial defence. The idea is that one pair of birds in one territory can frighten a pair of birds in an adjacent territory by engaging in a quartet. By singing in a quartet, each pair of birds is supposedly flinging insults at the other pair! However, there is a major problem with this theory. If duetting birds really want to insult their neighbours, then why do they bother to engage in extreme levels of co-operation to produce quartets of outstanding natural beauty? The beauty and precision of quartet bird song clearly reveals the hand of the Creator!

6.10 Admissions by evolutionists

The evidence of musical structure and beauty in the songs of birds has astonished and perplexed scientists who believe in evolution. Catchpole and Slater, who are currently leading authors in the field of bird song, have said:

…birds produce an astonishing variety of vocal sounds. These range from short, monosyllabic calls, to some of the longest and most complicated sounds known to science; Bird songs occur in a bewildering variety of forms, often extremely elaborate, and are as puzzling to explain as the plumage of a bird of paradise or a peacock's tail; At first sight, the diversity of modes of singing amongst birds is so great that it defies explanation. Many species, particularly the non-passerines, have relatively simple calls or songs. Clearly, they can get by without undue complexity, so why have some songbirds evolved such elaborate signals? Looking at repertoire sizes alone there are also enormous differences between songbird species: how can we attempt to explain [by evolution] such diversity?[17]

The simple answer to the final question in the above quotation is that evolution can never explain the existence and diversity of bird song because chance genetic mistakes can never produce sophisticated voice mechanisms or beautiful music.

Thorpe, who was a leading authority on bird song, says this about the duet songs of the African shrike:

In the shrike songs the 'form' or structure of the actual units is very close to—sometimes identical with—that produced by some of our musical instruments, notably the clarinet. The form of the whole songs comprising a preponderance of consonant intervals whose ratios occur at or near just intonation, will be almost by definition 'harmonious'. In some of the more elaborate duets the melodic line is based upon a major or minor triad. These and the many duets incorporating a falling major 3rd or a rising major 4th cannot help but give a strong impression of tonality especially when the rhythmic impulse is such that it gives prominence to an assumed key-note. To the musical listener these songs may seem over harmonious; nevertheless it is the kind of harmony to which man aspired and which probably reached its peak in Mozart. No musical listener could call the songs 'unmusical' or 'displeasing'; their only fault from our point of view rests in their brevity and simplicity.[18]

In this quotation Thorpe fully admits that the songs of the African shrike contain objective musical harmony and beauty.

Bird experts sometimes admit that the theory of evolution is incapable of explaining how bird song could have evolved. Thorpe has said the following:

In spite of all that has been said above in respect of the advantage for song birds of developing a high degree of complexity in their vocal utterances, we do find a great deal of elaboration which goes beyond anything which would seem to be biologically advantageous. The vocal gymnastic ability to be discussed in the final chapter is only one of these features. The nightingale's song is another instance in which the elaboration of pattern seems to have gone to quite excessive lengths, unless indeed we suppose that the listening bird has something approaching aesthetic appreciation…it is hard to imagine any selective reason for the extreme purity of some bird-notes…It is as if specialisation has gone in advance of immediate adaptive requirements.[19]

There are some very serious admissions in this quotation. According to evolution, specialisation can never go before adaptive requirements, yet the author admits that this is the only way he can explain bird song. If it is hard to imagine 'any selective reason for extreme purity', then surely this shows that there *is* no selective reason for such purity! If the elaboration in bird song is 'beyond anything which would seem to be biologically advantageous', then surely this is because it has been added deliberately. If the 'elaboration of pattern' in the song of the nightingale has gone to 'extreme lengths' then surely this shows added beauty!

6.11 Bird song in classical music

Bird song appears in classical music both in the quality of sound and also in the melody of the compositions. The flute in particular has a sound resembling that of a songbird. An example of bird song in classical music is found in Vivaldi's flute concerto No. 3 in D. This concerto is popularly known as *The goldfinch* because the music contains sounds which resemble the songs produced by the goldfinch. Birds such as the marsh warbler and chaffinch can sing a musical trill which is very common in classical music. In some ways, birds have a more sophisticated voice than musical instruments. For example, wind instruments can generally produce only one sound at a time, whereas a bird can produce two.

Other pieces of classical music that contain bird song include Handel's organ concerto No. 13 in F major which is popularly known as *The cuckoo and nightingale*, Leopold Mozart's *Toy symphony* and Prokofiev's *Peter and the wolf*. One of the most famous pieces for bird music is Beethoven's *Pastoral symphony*. In one section of the symphony the music slows right down and three birds are heard to sing: the nightingale is represented by the flute; the quail is represented by the oboe; and the cuckoo is represented by the clarinet. Beethoven was a great lover of the natural world and was no doubt inspired by bird song.

Probably the most common example of bird song in classical music is the sound of the cuckoo. The cuckoo produces a characteristic interval which can be interpreted as a major third or minor third depending on the musical context. These intervals are significant in music and this explains why the cuckoo sound is used so much in composition. Delius wrote an orchestral piece called *On hearing the first cuckoo in spring* which contains a prominent solo cuckoo sound. The French composer Daquin wrote a piano piece based on the sound of the cuckoo called *Le cuckoo*. The French composer Saint-Saens wrote an orchestral piece called the *Animal carnival* which includes a clear cuckoo interval. Beethoven's piano sonata No. 25 in G Major is popularly known as *The cuckoo*. The third movement of Beethoven's piano concerto No. 2 in B flat major also contains the characteristic cuckoo interval.

The most extensive copying of bird song in classical music was carried out by a French composer called Oliver Messiaen (1908–1992) who studied music at the Paris Conservatoire. Oliver Messiaen spent long hours making detailed studies of bird song and then wrote piano music based on the songs. In 1959 Messiaen published a set of piano pieces based on his recordings of bird song called *Catalogue d'Oiseaux* (Bird catalogue). This set of pieces contains music based on the songs of the following birds: alpine chough, golden oriole, blue rock thrush, black-eared wheatear, tawny owl, woodlark, reed warbler, short-toed lark, cetti's warbler, rock thrush, buzzard, black wheatear and curlew. Messiaen was a gifted musician who could recognise that bird song contained great musical merit. Messiaen said this about bird song:

I grasped the fact that there are many things which have not been invented by man, that there are many things in nature which simply exist around us. It is just that no one has paid attention to them. Men talk of scales and modes: the birds have scales and modes. There is much talk of the division of small tonal intervals: birds sing these intervals. Wagner had a great deal to say about leitmotiv: every bird is a living leitmotiv, for it has its own aesthetic and its own theme.[20]

Notice in this quotation how Messiaen admits that bird song possesses some of the same musical characteristics as those produced by human composers. In fact, Messiaen also admits that in nature 'there are many things which have not been invented by man'. Since man-made music has an intelligent composer, it is perfectly reasonable to assume that bird song has an intelligent divine Composer.

Bird song has not only inspired great composers of music but it has also inspired great poets. One of the most well known poems of the famous poet John Keats, entitled *Ode to a nightingale,* was written when he was in a garden listening to the song of that bird. Evolutionists believe that it is by chance accident that birds produce songs and intervals that are so beautiful that they have inspired the most brilliant composers and writers. However, a better explanation is surely that bird song has been designed and composed by an infinitely wise Creator.

6.12 The goodness of God in creation

The existence of bird song shows the obedience of birds to the exhortation: *'Let everything that has breath praise the Lord.' (Psalm 150:6).* Sadly, there are not many modern scientists who give praise to the Lord. It is very sad how the evolutionist will think of any reason for the existence of beauty as long it does not involve any conscious planning by a Creator. The evolutionist rejects any divine purpose in beautiful natural events like the dawn chorus. In contrast, a Christian can see purpose in the dawn chorus. The dawn chorus has been made to celebrate the beginning of a new day. The psalmist instructs us to rejoice in each new day: 'This is the day the Lord has made; we will rejoice and be glad in it.' (Psalm 118:24).

There is profound beauty in bird feathers and bird song and yet these are only two aspects of creation. There are many other parts of creation that could be studied in detail to show how there is wonderful beauty throughout nature. Jesus said, 'Consider the lilies of the field, how they grow: they neither toil nor spin: and yet I say to you that even Solomon in all his glory was not arrayed like one of these.' (Matthew 6:28–29). These verses describe how God has clothed the flowers of the field with great beauty. King Solomon was a rich king and would have been dressed in a very beautiful way. And yet the beauty of lilies exceeds the beauty of King Solomon.

God has put things in nature so that man can enjoy beauty with all his senses of sight, hearing, smell, touch and taste. The writer A.W. Pink said this about the goodness of God in providing beauty in the earth:

Our physical lives could have been sustained without beautiful flowers to regale our eyes with their colours, and our nostrils with their sweet perfumes. We might have walked the fields without our ears being saluted by the music of birds. Whence, then, this loveliness, this charm, so freely diffused over the face of nature? Verily, "The tender mercies of the Lord are over all His works" (Psalm 145:9). The goodness of God is seen in the variety of natural pleasures which He has provided for His creatures. God might have been pleased to satisfy our hunger without the food being pleasing to our palates- how His benevolence appears in the varied flavours which He has given to meats, vegetables, and fruits! God has not only given us senses, but also that which gratifies them; and this too reveals His goodness.[21]

Charles Spurgeon said this about God's wonderful provision of beauty:

God has made nature not only for our necessities, but also for our pleasures. He has not only made fields of corn, but he has created the violet and cowslip. Air alone would be sufficient for us to breathe, but see how He has loaded it with perfumes; bread alone might sustain life, but mark the sweet fruits with which nature's lap is brimming. The colours of flowers, the beauties of scenery, the music of birds, all show how the great Creator has cared for lawful gratification of every sense of man. Nor is it a sin to enjoy these gifts of heaven; but it would be folly to close one's soul to their charm.[22]

In this modern age we are so often surrounded by the images and noises produced by man-made technology and entertainment that we can be unaware of much of the beauty of nature. Also, the atheistic philosophy of the modern age does not inspire people to make a habit of studying natural beauty. However, the Christian should have a desire to study what God has consciously made. The reader is encouraged to spend time in the quiet of a garden or wood and to enjoy the wonderful beauty of creation such as bird song. There is no better entertainment than that which has been directly provided by the Creator. How we need to follow the advice of Elihu who told Job: 'Stand still and consider the wondrous works of God...' (Job 37:14).

Notes on Chapter 6

1   **Armstrong, E.A.,** *A study of bird song,* Oxford University Press, p. 35, 1963.

2   **Thorpe, W.H.,** *Bird-song: the biology of vocal communication and expression in birds,* Cambridge University Press, p. 5, 1961.

3   **Thorpe, W.H.,** 'Duetting and antiphonal song in birds', *Behaviour Supplement,* Vol 18, p. 148, 1972.

4   **Catchpole, C.K. and Slater, P.J.B.,** *Bird song,* Cambridge University Press, pp. 23–24, 1995.

5   **Catchpole, C.K.,** *op. cit.,* p. 28.

6   **Hartley, R.S.,** 'Expiratory muscle activity during song production in the canary', *Respir. Physiol.,* No 81, pp. 177–188, 1990.

7   **Catchpole, C.K.,** *op. cit.,* p. 165.

8   **Catchpole, C.K.,** *op. cit.,* p. 171.

9   *Daily Telegraph,* Thursday 17th May 2001.

10 **Armstrong, E.A.,** *op. cit.,* p. 30.

11 **Hinde, R.A.,** *Bird Vocalisation,* Cambridge University Press, p. 188, 1969.

12 **Catchpole, C.K.,** *op. cit.,* p. 11.

13 **Catchpole, C.K.,** *op. cit.,* p. 116.

14 **Catchpole, C.K.,** *op. cit.,* p. 122.

15 **Catchpole, C.K.,** *op. cit.,* p. 177.

16 **Catchpole, C.K.,** *op. cit.,* p. 174.

17 **Catchpole, C.K.,** *op. cit.,* p. 21, 140, 187.

18 **Thorpe, W.H. (1972),** *op. cit.,* pp. 159–160.

19 **Thorpe, W.H. (1961),** *op. cit.,* pp. 63–64.

20 Information sheet accompanying the CD by Martin Zehn (Piano), *Catalogue d'oiseaux,* Art Nova Classics, 2000.

21 **Pink, A.W.,** *The attributes of God,* Baker, p. 58, 1975.

22 **Spurgeon, C.H.,** *Autobiography Vol 2, The full harvest,* Banner of Truth, pp. 131–132, 1973.

Extreme similarity in features

The hearing ear and the seeing eye, The Lord has made them both (Proverbs 20:12).

There are remarkable similarities in the features of many different types of creature. The eye is one example of a feature which is very similar in several types of creature such as mammals, birds and fish. Such close similarity in widely different creatures can be called extreme similarity. This chapter defines extreme similarity and gives several striking examples of this type of similarity in nature.

Evolutionists believe that all creatures including human beings can be plotted on a single evolutionary tree and that the tree shows a progression from lower to higher life forms, as shown in Fig. 7–1. Virtually all biology books now teach that the similarities that exist in the features of different

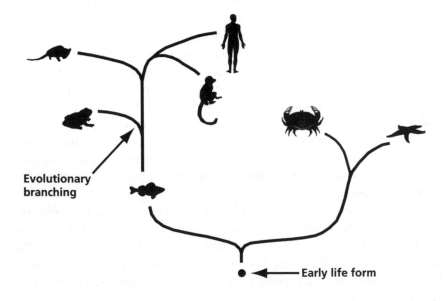

Evolutionary branching

Early life form

Fig. 7–1 Evolutionary tree as proposed by evolutionists

organisms provide evidence for this supposed evolutionary tree.[1] Charles Darwin said that he considered similarity to be so important that he would believe in evolution even if there was no other evidence.[2] The fact that organisms can be classified into groups, like mammals and amphibians, which have similar features, is also used as evidence for an evolutionary tree.

Despite the claims made in biology books, similarity by itself does *not* provide automatic evidence for evolution. The reason for this is that similarity of features is exactly what would be expected from a Designer. The fact that similarity is a natural by-product of intelligent design is demonstrated in the design of man-made devices like land vehicles. Vehicles such as trains, lorries, cars, motorbikes and bicycles have many similarities such as wheels, lights and windows.

However, the fact that land vehicles have similar features does not mean that they have evolved from each other. The similarities between land vehicles are due only to the fact that an intelligent designer deliberately uses similar solutions in different contexts. In fact, there are such unique features in different transport vehicles that it would be impossible for them to have evolved from each other. For example, motorbikes contain many complex mechanisms not found in bicycles and articulated lorries contain many complex mechanisms not found in motor cars.

The fact that land vehicles have similar features means that it is possible to produce a classification tree which groups together particular types of vehicle, as shown in Fig. 7–2. In fact, a classification tree can be produced for any type of man-made device such as gears, bearings, doors and windows. The reason why a classification tree can be produced for different kinds of man-made products is that these products have intelligent designers who plan similarity. In the same way, the similarity that exists in nature can be considered to be due to the existence of a common Designer.

The only way that similarity could be considered evidence for evolution is if the evolutionist could show that the similarity seen in nature is what would be expected from evolution *rather* than design. However, the evolutionist has not done this. The following sections show that in nature what we actually see is a type of similarity that can only be produced by intelligent design.

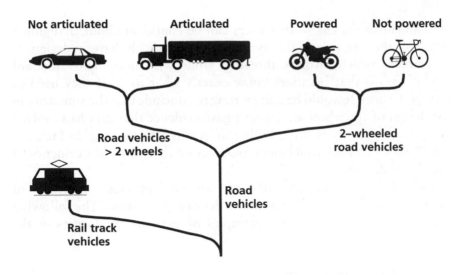

Fig. 7–2 Classification tree for land vehicles

7.1 Hallmark of design: extreme similarity in features

If creatures had evolved, there should be close similarity of features only in creatures that are of a similar type. For example, there is such a large distance between the branches of a human, a frog and an insect on the proposed evolutionary tree that one would not expect to find extreme similarities in features between them if they had evolved. Therefore, evolution is limited in the extent to which it could produce similarity of features.

In contrast to the process of evolution, there is no limit to the extent to which an intelligent designer can create similarity. Indeed, there are important reasons why human designers deliberately try to produce extreme similarity in products. For example, products are easier to understand and look after by users when there are standard features in them. Similarity between different products is so common in engineering design that there is a whole subject area on this called *standardisation and modularization.*[3]

An example of extreme similarity in engineering is found in car wheels. Car manufacturers deliberately design a very similar method of wheel attachment to the car so that users can be confident about changing a wheel if the car gets a flat tyre. Most car wheels have a design of attachment which involves threaded studs with nuts. This standard feature means that car users know exactly what to do if they need to change a wheel. It would be quite wrong to conclude that the similarity in the design of the wheel attachment gave evidence that cars had evolved when the similarity is actually due to intelligent planning. In fact, the similarities in wheel attachment are so close that this gives evidence of intelligent design.

Extreme similarity in different contexts provides evidence of intelligent design in both man-made devices and nature. The following sections give several striking examples of extreme similarities in the natural world.

7.2 Land and sea mammals

According to the theory of evolution, life started in a primitive sea and, as creatures became more advanced, they moved to the land and then the air. Therefore, if life had evolved, one would expect the sea to contain mostly so-called 'primitive' life forms and the land and air to contain mostly 'advanced' life forms. For example, mammals are considered to be an advanced life form that evolved after creatures supposedly adapted to land. Mammals have an internal skeleton, they keep a constant body temperature and they breathe air through lungs. However, what actually exists in nature contradicts what would be expected from evolution because mammals are found on land *and* in water *and* in the air. An example of a mammal in these different environments is the horse, the whale and the bat respectively.

It is very difficult for evolution to explain why some mammals appear to have moved from the land back to the sea to become whales whilst others supposedly evolved to become flying creatures! In contrast, the presence of very similar mammalian features in land, water and flying creatures is just what would be expected from a common Designer. Another problem with the theory of evolution is that there is no such thing as a primitive creature. All creatures, whether they are fish, insects, mammals or bacteria, are immensely complicated and supremely well designed for their environment.

7.3 Marsupial and placental mammals

There are three types of mammals: monotremes, marsupials and placental mammals. The monotremes are egg-laying mammals and there are only a few known living species including the platypus. The marsupials develop their offspring inside the mother's womb and these are born at a very early stage of development. Following birth, a marsupial offspring like a baby kangaroo will live in the marsupial pouch until it is strong enough to live away from its mother. There are many types of marsupial mammals presently living in Australia. In the case of placental mammals, offspring are developed with a placenta within the mother's womb and this enables the offspring to grow to an advanced stage before birth. Placental mammals are the most common type of mammal and they include the human being.

If life had evolved, little similarity could be expected between the external features of these three different types of mammal since they have such vastly different methods of reproduction. The amount of time required to evolve such differences in the reproductive system would be so great that the rest of the animal would inevitably change significantly. Indeed, the evolutionist commonly refers to monotremes and marsupials as primitive compared to placental mammals. However, despite what would be expected from evolution, the reality is that there are incredible similarities in the external features of the different types of mammal.

The similarities between marsupial and placental mammals have been studied by Batten[4] and some of his examples are summarised in Table 7–1. Some of the mammals in Table 7–1 are so similar that it is difficult to tell if they are marsupial or placental without a close inspection. For example, some types of marsupial mouse look almost identical to the placental mouse. Only by looking for a pouch can the type of mammal be determined. The evolutionist tries to overcome the problem of similar features with theories like the 'convergence theory' which states that a creature will converge on a common design solution. However, there is no reason why features such as size, shape, fur, facial details and limb structure should be so similar in both marsupial and placental mammals. The existence of extreme similarities between marsupial and placental mammals gives strong evidence of deliberate design.

Table 7–1 Marsupial and placental mammals with similar features

MARSUPIALS	PLACENTALS
Feathertail glider	Flying squirrel
Marsupial mouse	Mouse
Cuscus	Monkey
Marsupial mole	Golden mole
Quoll	Cat
Bilby	Hare
Rat kangaroo	Rat
Wombat	Marmot
Numbat	Anteater

7.4 Creatures which extract nectar

Birds, mammals and insects are very different classes of creature and yet there are great similarities in the way that creatures in each class can extract nectar from flowers. The hummingbird has a very long tongue and an ability to hover over flowers so that it can extract nectar. The greater long-nosed bat is also supremely well designed to extract nectar from flowers because it has a long nose and long tongue and can hover like a hummingbird. During the day, the greater long-nosed bat roosts in caves in large colonies. The bats come out at night to feed on the nectar and pollen in flowers of desert plants such as agaves. They also help the agave plants reproduce by spreading pollen.

Many insects can also hover over flowers and extract nectar. The hummingbird hawk moth is so named because it has remarkable similarities with a hummingbird in the way it hovers and uses a long tongue to extract nectar. The hummingbird hawk moth has a grey body and a black tail with white spots at the end. When people see a hummingbird hawk moth, they often think they have seen a hummingbird because of the striking similarities in appearance and behaviour. Considering how difficult it is for a creature to hover and extract nectar, it is remarkable that three completely separate classes of flying creature can perform these feats.

7.5 Creatures with common names

Many creatures in widely different classes of organism have remarkable similarities in external features such as coloration, body shape or body armour. Sometimes the features are so similar that creatures in one class of animal are named after a creature from another class of animal. Some examples of shared names are shown in Table 7–2. The fact that there are many creatures that share names provides evidence that a common Designer has designed them all.

Table 7–2 Shared names in different types of creature

CREATURE	CREATURE WITH SIMILAR FEATURES
Leopard	Leopard lizard, leopard seal, leopard tortoise
Zebra	Zebra fish, zebra finch
Tiger	Tiger moth
Horse	Sea horse
Owl	Owl butterfly
Peacock	Peacock butterfly
Hummingbird	Hummingbird hawk moth
Porcupine	Porcupine fish
Duck	Duck-billed platypus
Giraffe	Giraffe beetle
Rhino	Rhino beetle

7.6 Warning colours and patterns

Some creatures in nature possess a colour scheme which identifies them as distasteful or poisonous creatures to potential predators. When predators see such creatures, the visual warning signal is recognised and the predator leaves the creatures alone. Such visual warning is called aposematic coloration. Common warning colours are black, yellow, red and white and common warning patterns are stripes and spots. There is often a remarkable consistency in the visual warning signs of creatures which are from different classes. For example, the coral snake and some arrow-poison frogs have a remarkable similarity in their black, yellow and red markings. Of course, the evolutionist claims that such common coloration has evolved because it has become the accepted colour scheme by predators, but the existence of such similarity in different contexts requires intelligent planning.

Some creatures have a colour warning sign even though they are not poisonous. The reason why such deceptive warning signs can work is that these creatures look very similar to other creatures which *are* poisonous. For example, the viceroy butterfly is a non-poisonous butterfly which has a remarkable similarity in coloration to the poisonous monarch butterfly. The king snake is a non-poisonous snake which looks very similar to the coral snake. The hoverfly is a non-poisonous insect which looks similar to the wasp. Such similarities again give evidence of design.

7.7 Faces in different types of creature

Some of the main features of the face are the eyes, ears, nose and mouth. If life had evolved, one would expect to find great variation in the facial features of different creatures. The reason for this is that there are such large differences between the different classes of creature such as reptiles and mammals that one would expect their faces also to be very different.

Despite the logical outcome of evolution, however, there is actually an amazing consistency in the layout of the face of the human being and different types of creature, as shown in Fig. 7–3. Virtually all mammals have two eyes, two ears, one nose, one mouth and one tongue. Virtually all fish, insects, reptiles, mammals and birds have two eyes and one mouth. The existence of a very small number of four-eyed creatures such as the four-eyed fish and the four-eyed beetle does not change the conclusion about the similarity of faces because these creatures actually have two eyes with each eye divided into two parts. One part is for looking out of water and one for looking into water. Therefore, the term four-eyed refers to function and not appearance.

Fig. 7–3 Similar facial layouts in different species

The fact that most insects have two compound eyes is particularly remarkable because they have a completely different type of eye to mammals. Insects have numerous mini-eyes called *ommatidia* that are grouped together into two compound eyes on the sides of the head. The fact that the numerous mini-eyes of insects are specially grouped together to form two eyes provides evidence of deliberately planned similarity. It is interesting to note that butterflies sometimes have the appearance of eyes on their wings. For example, the owl butterfly is so named because it has a remarkable resemblance to the eyes of an owl. The peacock butterfly also has the appearance of eyes. Such patterns are not surprising if the same Creator has made all creatures.

Recent experiments in the field of genetics have shown that it does not take many molecular adjustments to make drastic changes to the layout of the face. In December 2001 there was a report in the journal *Nature*[5] of how scientists produced a chick with two beaks after carrying out a relatively small number of molecular changes to the embryo of the developing chick. It is very difficult for evolution to explain why all the millions of different species of creature on the earth have such a similar layout of the face if they have evolved by random accidents over millions of years. The similarity of faces in nature gives powerful evidence of conscious design!

7.8 Limb structure in different types of creature

There are remarkable similarities between humans and other creatures in the positioning and structure of the body and limbs. For example, humans have two bones in the forearm and lower leg and one bone between the elbow and shoulder and between the knee and hip. This limb positioning and structure is extremely similar to the layout found in creatures as different as horses and bats. Of course, the evolutionist uses this similarity to claim that humans have evolved from so-called 'primitive' life forms. However, the similarities are so close that they actually give evidence of deliberate design. This is because there are such diverse features in the animal kingdom that one would expect that the bone positioning and structure would also be very varied if evolution had occurred.

Similarity of limbs was one of the main aspects of nature that encouraged Darwin to propose the theory of evolution. Darwin said:

What can be more curious than that the hand of a man, formed for grasping, that of a mole for digging, the leg of a horse, the paddle of the porpoise, and the wing of the bat should all be constructed on the same pattern and should include similar bones, and in the same relative positions?[6]

What Darwin did not realise is that the similarities are so extreme that they can only be explained by deliberate design!

7.9 Extreme similarities in DNA

There is a remarkable similarity in the structure of the DNA molecule in animals and plants and even micro-organisms. Many evolutionists claim that this similarity is evidence that organisms are related by evolution. They believe that human beings are only human because they have a few genes that differentiate them from other animals. However, the similarity in DNA in different organisms is so extreme that it is much more an evidence of deliberate design than of evolution. It is interesting that some evolutionists admit that the extreme similarity in DNA can be an evidence of deliberate design. For example, M. Ridley, who is the chairman of the International Centre for Life (UK) says:

No life form exists without DNA… in my view no one has made enough of the fact that the three letter-words of the genetic code are the same in every creature… Wherever you go, whatever animal, plant, bug or blob you look at, if it is alive it will use the same dictionary and know the same code. It means—and religious people might find this a useful argument—that there was only one creation, one single event when life was born.[7]

The DNA molecule does indeed represent a very useful argument. It provides powerful evidence that all organisms have a common Designer and that the common Designer is God!

7.10 Great scientists and similarity

There have been great scientists who have seen similarity not as an evidence of evolution but as an evidence of design. The famous scientist James Clerk Maxwell used similarity as an argument to refute evolution. In a paper he sent to the British Association for the advancement of science, Maxwell wrote:

No theory of evolution can be formed to account for the similarity of molecules, for evolution necessarily implies continuous change... The exact equality of each molecule to all others of the same kind gives it...the essential character of a manufactured article.[8]

Carl Linnaeus was a botanist who was one of the key scientists who developed the system for classifying plants and animals. Linnaeus used a branching system to divide the plant and animal kingdoms into large groups called classes. Classes were then broken down into orders and orders were broken down into divisions called genera (genera is plural for genus). Despite formulating a logical classification tree, Linnaeus did not believe that this pointed towards evolution. As with man-made devices, classification of natural species is just what would be expected from design.

Georges Cuvier was one of the key scientists who established the science of comparative anatomy and palaeontology. As its name suggests, comparative anatomy is the science of comparing similar anatomical structures in different creatures but Cuvier saw this similarity as evidence of design and not evolution. Palaeontology is the science of fossils but Cuvier again saw this as providing no evidence for evolution.

It is ironic that many modern scientists quote classification trees, comparative anatomy and palaeontology as evidence for evolution,[9] when the main founding scientists of these subjects were actually strong supporters of biblical creation!

7.11 The goodness of God in creation

God has shown His goodness towards man by making creatures have similar features to man, such as the face, so that man can see that creatures have a common maker and so that man can relate to animals. Similarities also make it easier for man to look after animals because similar procedures can be used on animals by vets and farmers. For example, when animals give birth to offspring, similar procedures can be used to look after the mothers and their offspring. Also, if an animal receives an injury to a limb, standard procedures can be used to nurse the limb because of the similarities in the design of limb in different animals. Vets and farmers can also become familiar with common symptoms when animals get ill.

God also showed love towards mankind by giving Adam and Eve the task of filling the earth with people. He could easily have filled the earth with people Himself but there were good reasons why He let man do it by procreation. By enabling people to reproduce, this causes them to feel closely related to each other and to have the joy of seeing similarities in others. In his Genesis commentary, John Calvin says this about human procreation:

God could himself have covered the earth with a multitude of men; but it was his will that we should proceed from one fountain, in order that our desire of mutual concord might be the greater, and that each might the more freely embrace the other as his own flesh.[10]

It is interesting to note that gene variation is an ideal way of producing differences in the appearance of offspring, especially in the case of human beings. On the one hand, if there was no gene variation, then there would be the very undesirable situation where everyone looked identical! On the other hand, if there was too much variation in genes, then children would not have similarities with their parents and would not feel closely related to them. In reality, gene variation produces enough variety to make everyone appear different, but enough similarity to make people feel related. It is ironic that similarity is so often quoted as evidence of evolution when in reality it is evidence of design and of the infinite goodness of God! The psalmist reminds us of God's goodness towards mankind in this verse: '...The earth is full of the goodness of the Lord!' (Psalm 33:5).

Notes on Chapter 7

1   **Roberts, M.B.V.,** *Biology a functional approach*, 4th Ed. Nelson, p. 570, 1986.

2   **Darwin, C.** (1872), *Origin of Species*, 6th Ed., Collier books, New York, p. 457, 1962.

3   **Pahl, G., and Beitz, W.,** *Engineering design: a systematic approach*, 2nd Edition, Springer Verlag, p. 433, 1996.

4   **Batten. D.,** 'Are look-a-likes related?', *Creation* 19(2), pp. 39–41, March-May 1997.

5   **S.-H. Lee, K. K. FU, J. N. Hui & J. M. Richman, '**Noggin and retinoic acid transform the identity of avian facial prominences', *Nature* 414, pp. 909–912, 2001.

6   Quoted from **Hinchliffe, J.R. and Johnson, D.R.,** *The development of the vertebrate limb*, Clarendon Press, inside cover, 1980.

7   **Ridley, M.,** 'Genome', *Daily Telegraph,* August 23, 1999.

8   **Lamont, A.,** *21 Great Scientists who believed*, Creation Science Foundation, p. 207, 1995.

9   **Roberts, M.B.V.,** *op. cit.,* p. 575.

10 **Calvin, J.,** *Genesis*, Banner of Truth, Genesis 1:28, p. 97, 1965.

Extreme diversity of kinds

O Lord, how manifold are Your works! In wisdom You
have made them all. The earth is full of Your
possessions—this great and wide sea, in which are
innumerable teeming things, living things both small and
great (Psalm 104:24–25).

T he natural world contains a spectacular diversity of life. There are
many different types of organism to be found in virtually every
environment of the earth. Organisms also come in a great variety
of shapes and sizes. This chapter defines extreme diversity and gives
several remarkable examples of this type of diversity in nature.

One reason for diversity in nature is that there is *variation* within each
basic kind of creature. For example, there are many different types of dog
due to the great genetic potential of the dog kind. A second reason for
diversity in nature is that there are many different *kinds* of living organism
in the earth. Evolutionists claim that the diversity of basic kinds of creature
is evidence of evolution[1] because it is supposedly possible to imagine an
evolutionary progression from simple creatures to complex creatures. For
example, evolutionists claim that the existence of single-celled organisms
provides evidence that all life came from this 'primitive' state. However,
diversity is just what one would expect from a Creator, so it is wrong to
automatically associate diversity with evolution. Man-made design
demonstrates that diversity is a natural by-product of intelligent design.
For example, there are many different types of car such as the saloon,
sports, estate, hatchback, 4x4 and people-mover. The reason for the wide
variety of cars is not because cars have evolved but because designers have
deliberately designed different cars for different environments and
applications. Since diversity is a natural by-product of intelligent design, it
is wrong to assume that diversity is an evidence of evolution.

The only way that diversity could be considered evidence for evolution is if the evolutionist could show that the diversity seen in nature is what would be expected from evolution *rather* than design. However, the evolutionist has not done this. The following sections show that in nature what we actually see is a type of diversity that can only be produced by design and not evolution.

8.1 Hallmark of design: extreme diversity of kinds

According to the theory of evolution, the process of evolution is able to produce many different kinds of creature. However, because evolution works by incremental change, the process of evolution could only ever produce a variety which fitted within an evolutionary tree where there were small differences between the different types of organism in the tree. Evolution could not produce a unique kind of creature or plant that had several different features to any other creature or plant that has ever existed. Also, it could not produce unique processes in a creature or plant that were completely different to other processes that have existed in nature. Evolution is also limited in the extent to which it could fill different ecological niches. For example, it would be impossible for creatures or plants to adapt to extreme environments if this required the existence of complex mechanisms that had never existed before. Therefore, the process of evolution could only ever produce a limited diversity.

In contrast to the process of evolution, there is no limit to the extent to which an intelligent designer can create diversity. Indeed, there are important reasons why human designers deliberately plan extreme diversity in products. In the case of cars, extreme diversity is produced in order to demonstrate the skill of the designers and also to satisfy the desire of car enthusiasts. For example, there are some extreme types of cars such as racing cars, solar-powered cars and rally cars. These cars contain unique and specialised mechanisms which are not found on normal cars. To design these extreme types of car requires a great deal of ingenuity and planning on the part of the designers. These cars represent clear evidence of intelligent design because they have such unique features.

Since evolution is limited in the extent to which it could produce diversity, *extreme diversity* is an exclusive hallmark of intelligent design. The following sections describe how there is abundant evidence of extreme diversity in the natural world.

8.2 Hummingbirds

Hummingbirds are a type of bird which can hover around flowers and extract nectar. Nectar is the main energy source for hummingbirds but they also eat insects for protein. A hummingbird is so named because its wings flap so fast that it often generates an audible and characteristic 'hum'. There are over 300 species of hummingbird but they all have a similar structure. Hummingbirds live in the Western Hemisphere from Canada to Southern Chile. The majority of hummingbird species are found in the tropics in countries like Equador. The smallest hummingbird is the bee hummingbird which has an adult length of about 5cm (length from bill to tail). The largest hummingbird is the giant hummingbird which has an adult length of about 20cm. Most male hummingbirds have brightly coloured and iridescent feathers.

Hummingbirds are a good example of extreme diversity because they have a unique design and perform very sophisticated forms of flight. A hummingbird can perform some amazing aerial feats including vertical take-off, precision hovering and backwards flight. The special features of hummingbirds are briefly explained in the following sections:

I SPECIAL WING STRUCTURE

Hummingbirds have a unique wing structure where the elbow and wrist joints are fixed. This wing structure makes each wing act like a stiff, powerful paddle. The shoulder joint is extremely flexible and this enables the hummingbird to put the wings into many different positions for different forms of flight. There are huge wing muscles that produce powerful flight and these muscles represent up to 40 per cent of the bird's total body weight.

II SPECIAL WING MOVEMENT

The unique wing structure of hummingbirds enables them to perform extraordinary wing movements which are unique to this type of bird. A

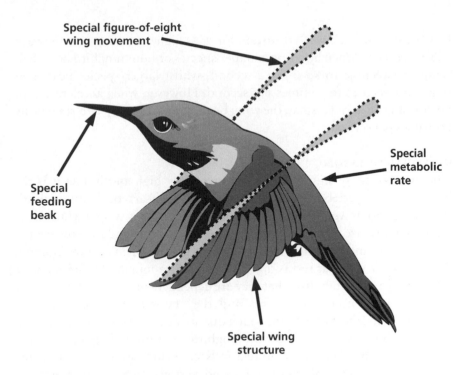

Special figure-of-eight wing movement

Special metabolic rate

Special feeding beak

Special wing structure

Fig. 8–1 Special features in the hummingbird

picture of a hovering hummingbird is shown in Fig. 8–1. With other birds, the wing movement is up and down and lift is only generated on the down stroke. However, with hummingbirds, the wing movement is not up and down but forwards and backwards. This unique movement enables hummingbirds to generate lift on both forward and backward strokes of the wing. There are three main forms of flight for hummingbirds: hovering, forward flight and backward flight. In hovering, the wings move in a figure-of-eight pattern and this enables the bird's body to be held stationary, vertically, horizontally or obliquely. The figure-of-eight motion is important because it has the consequence that the wings do not produce dead spots. This means that the forward and return paths of the wing do not overlap and hence they produce lift throughout the whole wing cycle. In backward flight, the wings are moved in a circular path above the bird's head to achieve backwards thrust. In forward flight, the wings also move in a circular path. When hovering, smaller species of hummingbird beat their wings between 40 to 80 times a second, whilst larger species beat their wings between 20 to 40 times per second. However, when accelerating or performing an aerial display, the wing beats can increase up to a staggering 200 times per second.

III SPECIAL METABOLIC RATE

The metabolism of hummingbirds is incredibly high and in fact it is the highest of all vertebrates by a long way. The heart of hummingbirds represents about two to three per cent of their total body weight which is the largest relative size of any animal. The heart beats at around 250–500 beats a minute at rest and rises to up to 1,200 beats a minute when the bird is active. The respiratory rate at rest is up to 250 breaths a minute. Hummingbirds have such a high metabolism that they are dependent on the very high energy content of the nectar of flowers and they need to be feeding almost continually. In fact, each day they eat a quantity of food equal to about half their own body weight! Some hummingbirds perform a daily hibernation routine to enable them to live in relatively cool climates. For example, the Andean hillstar hummingbird can spend periods each day in a state of hibernation with a colder body temperature in order to save energy.

IV SPECIAL FEEDING TUBE

Hummingbirds have a long tongue for reaching into flowers for nectar. The tongue laps up the nectar in a similar way to which a cat laps up food.

In many respects, hummingbirds are very different to other birds. This is how the keeper of tropical birds at London Zoo describes the hummingbird:

A hummingbird may be better depicted as a hybrid helicopter/jet fighter which has a huge, highly tuned and fuel-injected engine. The structure of the wing of the hummingbird is quite unlike that of every other of the 9,000 or so bird species.[2]

Notice here how the keeper describes the structure of the hummingbird's wing as being 'unlike that of every other of the 9,000 species of bird'.

Evolution cannot explain how a forward flying bird could suddenly become a bird that instantly possessed all of the complex apparatus necessary for hovering and extracting nectar from flowers. Without the complete hovering capability and feeding capability, a would-be hummingbird would perish. The hummingbird is so different to other types of bird that it is impossible for the evolutionist to hypothesise how it could fit onto any evolutionary tree.

There are some parallels between a harrier jump jet and the hummingbird since they can both hover and perform very advanced aerial feats. The harrier jump jet represents a unique type of aircraft and it took the creative efforts of talented engineers to design it. For example, the moveable power unit of the harrier is unique and incapable of being evolved from anything else. In the same way that a harrier cannot be evolved, so a hummingbird could not have evolved. However, the uniqueness of the hummingbird is just what would be expected from a Creator who intended the earth to contain a great diversity of life.

8.3 The camel

Deserts are largely made up of sand and rock and represent a severe environment because of the dryness and lack of vegetation. In addition, deserts are often very hot in the day and very cold at night and this makes it difficult for creatures to regulate their body temperature. Another severe problem with deserts is that sand is very abrasive and during a sandstorm, sand particles can do great damage to delicate body parts like the eyes and nose. Considering that deserts have such a severe environment, it is very remarkable that there are creatures and plants that actually thrive there. These creatures can only survive in the desert because they have special systems that are supremely well designed for desert conditions. Desert animals include the camel, kangaroo, lynx, coyote, hamster, roadrunner, kit fox, fennec fox, big horned sheep and addax. Desert birds include the elf owl, McQueen buzzard, Gambel's quail, red-tailed hawk and gila woodpecker. Desert reptiles and insects include the western rattlesnake, collared lizard, bull snake and desert beetle.

There are two species of camel living today: the dromedary and the bactrian. The dromedary camel has one hump and long legs and lives in the deserts of Arabia and Africa. The shorter bactrian camel has two humps with a very thick coat and lives in northern Asia, China and Afghanistan. Both types of camel are supremely well designed for desert conditions. The camel has been named the ship of the desert because it can walk across sand without difficulty and can go without drinking water for two weeks in hot weather. In cooler months the camel can go many weeks without drinking! To survive desert conditions the camel has several special features, as shown in Fig. 8–2. The following sections describe the special features of the camel:

I SPECIAL VARIABLE BODY TEMPERATURE

The body temperature of the human being must be kept very close to 37° C to avoid serious harm. However, the body temperature of the camel is

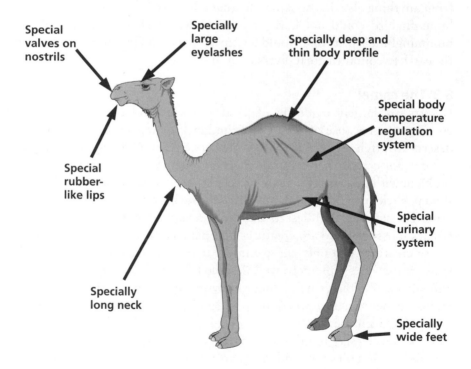

Special valves on nostrils

Specially large eyelashes

Specially deep and thin body profile

Special body temperature regulation system

Special rubber-like lips

Special urinary system

Specially long neck

Specially wide feet

Fig. 8–2 Special features in the camel

remarkable because it can vary by several degrees without the camel suffering ill effects. At night the temperature of the camel drops by a few degrees so that the camel does not feel so cold, whereas during the day the temperature of the camel rises by a few degrees so that it does not feel so hot. The camel's amazing variable body temperature helps to reduce sweating and hence to retain water.

II SPECIAL SLIM-LINE BODY

The camel has an especially slim body with most of its fat on top of its back. The narrow shape of the body is ideal for the desert because there is not much area for the sun to shine on especially at midday when the sun is highest in the sky.

III SPECIAL URINARY SYSTEM

The camel has an amazing ability to produce very concentrated urine in order to save water in hot weather.

IV SPECIAL DRINKING CAPACITY

When the camel is able to drink water, it can drink over 100 litres in just 10 minutes! The storage of such a large quantity of water is vital for enabling the camel to survive for long periods in the desert.

V SPECIAL WIDE FEET

Camels have special wide feet to prevent them sinking in soft sand. Without such feet, walking on sand would be very tiring, which is why horses are of limited use in the desert.

VI SPECIAL NOSTRILS

Camels have special valves that can close the nostrils down to tiny slits in the event of a sandstorm to prevent abrasive sand getting into the nose.

VII SPECIAL EYES

Camels have enormous eyelashes that shield the eyes from sand in a sandstorm. They also have an extra eyelid underneath the normal eyelid which is used to remove sand from the eyes. The extra eyelid moves from side to side like a car windscreen wiper. The extra eyelid is very thin, so that the camel can see through it. During a sandstorm, the camel opens its normal eyelids but closes its extra eyelids so that it can safely keep looking where it is going!

VIII SPECIAL MOUTH
Camels have a special mouth that is very flexible in order to cope with the prickly vegetation that grows in the desert.

IX SPECIAL LONG NECK
The camel has a long neck that helps it reach vegetation in awkward places.

X SPECIAL LONG LEGS
The camel has long legs to keep its body away from the ground where it is hot.

This brief survey of the camel shows that it is wonderfully designed and made for the desert. The evolutionist believes that the camel was a type of horse that evolved its special features in order to adapt to a changing environment. However, the special features of a camel require many precise design details that all have to be in place simultaneously for the camel to be able to survive in desert conditions. The camel is no accident but is evidence of conscious design.

8.4 The platypus
The platypus is a monotreme mammal which lives by rivers in Australia. A picture of a platypus is shown in Fig. 8–3. The platypus is an excellent diver and can stay under water for up to 14 minutes. The platypus has many unusual features that make it very different to virtually all other mammals. For example, apart from two spiny anteaters, the platypus is the only mammal to lay eggs. Having produced offspring in eggs, the platypus then goes on to feed the young with milk like a normal mammal. However, the platypus does not have feeding nipples but milk seeps out of pores in its skin! The platypus has such an unusual muzzle that it is sometimes called a duck-billed platypus because of the resemblance of its bill to that of a duck. The platypus also has webbed feet. The webs on the feet extend

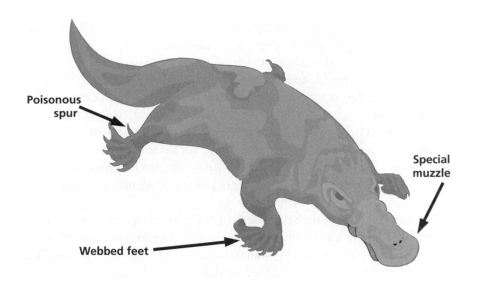

Poisonous
spur

Special
muzzle

Webbed feet

Fig. 8–3 Special features in the platypus

beyond the claws for swimming but can then be folded up when the animal is on land. The male platypus also has a defence system with poisonous spurs on its back legs which is unique in mammals.

The platypus is so unique that it is very difficult for the evolutionist to hypothesise any evolutionary ancestry. However, the uniqueness of the platypus is what would be expected from a Designer who wanted to produce extreme variety in the natural world.

8.5 The ginkgo tree

So far, this chapter has concentrated on unique features in creatures. However, there are also unusual plants that have such unique features that they provide evidence of design. One example of a plant with unique features is the ginkgo biloba tree. The ginkgo tree has fan-shaped leaves, as shown in Fig. 8–4(b). The tree produces yellowish, plumlike seeds about 2.5cm long, consisting of a 'nut' with a fleshy outer layer. The tree grows to about 30 to 40m in height. The ginkgo tree was discovered in the seventeenth century in Japan and it was later also found to be living in China. In the early eighteenth century it was brought to Europe and it can now be found all over the world. The ginkgo tree can have a very long life span. In China, some ginkgo trees are reported to be over 3,500 years old. The word ginkgo comes from the Chinese word 'yin kuo' which means silver fruit.

One of the unique features of the ginkgo tree are the leaves. There are thousands of different types of tree which grow leaves with a central midrib and branch-like veins, as shown in Fig. 8–4(a). However, the ginkgo tree is the only known living tree to have fan-shaped leaves. The fan-shaped leaves are distinctly different to a normal leaf and yet there is no evidence of any intermediate leaves. In fact, fossil evidence of ginkgo trees, which are supposedly millions of years old, reveals a virtually identical design of leaf to that of modern ginkgo biloba trees.

It is interesting to note that the leaf of the ginkgo tree has a remarkable resemblance to the leaf of the maidenhair fern. In fact, the resemblance is so great that the ginkgo tree is sometimes called the maidenhair tree. The similarity in leaf shape is used as evidence that the ginkgo tree is an intermediate plant between ferns and flowering plants such as trees. However, the ginkgo tree has all the characteristics of a tree such as a great size and strong trunk and is therefore not an intermediate type of plant.

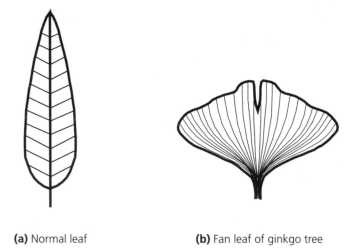

(a) Normal leaf   (b) Fan leaf of ginkgo tree

Fig. 8–4 The unique leaf of the ginkgo tree

The remarkable similarity between the leaf of the maidenhair fern and the ginkgo tree is an evidence of extreme similarity which indicates that the fern and the ginkgo tree have a common Designer.

Another very unusual feature of the ginkgo tree is the method of reproduction. Trees are generally flowering plants (angiosperms) which means that the seed is enclosed in a ripened fruit. However, the ginkgo is a gymnosperm, meaning 'naked seed', because the seed is protected by cones or a fleshy seed coat. Conifers are the only other type of tree to have such a method of carrying a seed. However, conifer trees are very different to the ginkgo tree. Whereas the ginkgo tree has deciduous leaves, conifers have needles. Ginkgo trees are also dioecious which means that the tree grows as separate male and female trees and the female tree must be growing in the presence of a male tree to be fertilized.

The ginkgo tree has the special status of being a single species, in a single genus, in a single family, in a single class, in a single phylum![3] Such a unique classification provides powerful evidence that the ginkgo tree is indeed unique. The ginkgo tree is just what would be expected from a Designer who wanted to produce extreme diversity.

8.6 Desert plants

Desert plants must be specially designed to survive the heat and drought of a desert. Some plants like cacti store large amounts of water in thick, fleshy leaves that have a waxy coat to prevent moisture leaking into the air. Desert plants often have hairs on their leaves to protect them from the drying wind. Cacti also have prickly spines to make it difficult for animals to eat them. Desert plants have special root systems that are either very deep or very spread out to capture as much water as possible. According to evolution, these desert plants gradually adapted to the desert conditions. However, desert plants are so different from other types of plants that they represent evidence of design.

8.7 Sophisticated physical processes

There are several special and unique physical processes in creatures for sensing and other purposes. These physical processes include magnetism, radar, electricity and luminescence. Such physical processes are very sophisticated and cannot be evolved from other physical processes such as digestion or metabolism. Indeed, it has taken humans many years of hard research to discover these special physical processes. Therefore, it is astounding that we find all of these physical processes already in creatures! The following sections describe some of the animals that have these special physical processes:

I MAGNETISM

Studies by Indiana University[4] have shown that leatherback turtles can navigate along a very narrow south-west corridor through the Pacific Ocean when migrating from Costa Rica to islands in the Pacific Ocean. The turtles always navigate within a corridor that is less than 100 miles in width. Considering the size of the Pacific Ocean, this is a very narrow channel! Scientists at Indiana University found that when magnetic decoy signals were given to a specific group of turtles, these turtles just swam in circles, unable to find their migratory route. It is a mystery to scientists how a creature like a turtle can contain a sensor that is able to detect the earth's magnetic field. It is very difficult for evolution to explain how an animal can evolve a magnetic sensor, let alone how baby turtles can be born with a precise navigation route in their heads!

II ULTRASOUND RADAR

The ultrasound radar system used by bats is also a very sophisticated sensor. Bats send out a high frequency sound and monitor how this ultrasound is reflected by surrounding objects. In order to detect the position of objects, the bat has to compensate for its own speed and direction of flight. A bat's radar is so sophisticated that a bat can fly fast around trees and other objects in darkness. It is very difficult for evolution to explain how a bat could evolve an ultrasound radar because the radar has to work perfectly and be fully integrated with the bat's brain to be of any use.

III ELECTRICITY

The South American electric eel is capable of electric shocks of up to 600 volts which is more than enough to electrocute very sizeable prey! This eel has organs consisting of stacks of sheet-like electroplates which are modified muscle fibres integrated with the nervous system. Usually a muscle contracts when it receives a nervous impulse. However, in the electric fish, the muscles send electrical impulses out of the body. There are also rays and catfish that have a similar ability to produce electric shocks. A great deal of effort and inventiveness was required by scientists to discover physical effects like electricity. Electricity could never have been discovered by making random changes to mechanical machinery. In the same way, electricity could not have simply appeared by chance in nature, especially in three different types of creature.

IV LUMINESCENCE

Luminescence is common in deep-sea fish but occurs elsewhere, for example in glow-worms. Luminescence is produced in special cells by an extremely complicated chemical reaction which involves the oxidation of an organic compound. In the case of the shrimp, there is even a reflecting layer behind the light-emitting cells and a special lens to concentrate the light. It is very difficult for evolution to explain how a creature could evolve luminescence because the whole chemistry for it has to be in place for it to be of any use.

V CHEMICAL REACTIONS

Powerful chemical reactions such as combustion are another type of important physical effect and these are also seen in the natural world. Combustion is defined as the mixing of a substance with oxygen that produces heat, light and a flame. The bombardier beetle has a powerful combustion system that can generate hot and noxious gases. It has two storage chambers inside its body that store two chemicals: hydroquinone and hydrogen peroxide dissolved in water. The beetle adds a further chemical called an inhibitor which prevents the hydrogen peroxide from oxidising the hydroquinone. When bombardier beetles are threatened, they squirt the chemicals from the storage chambers into two combustion tubes, together with another chemical that acts as a catalyst, to make a reaction. This happens very quickly and enough pressure is built up to squirt out the hot, noxious gas at high speed through a tube. All of these things happen under the precise control of the nervous system of the beetle. The bombardier beetle is just a tiny insect about one centimetre long, yet it has a cannon system that is even more elaborate than a rocket propulsion system! It is very difficult for evolution to explain how the beetle could have developed its chemical reaction system because all of the chemicals and control systems are needed simultaneously. Indeed, the presence of only some of the chemicals could result in a very dangerous scenario for the beetle itself!

8.8 Extreme range of habitats

There are many living organisms in some of the most remote and hostile places on earth such as the Arctics, remote coastal cliffs, the deep sea and even volcanoes. These creatures contain an astonishing level of optimum design. For example, the emperor penguin lives all year round on the pack ice of the Antarctic in temperatures as low as −62°C and with winds up to hurricane force. These tough penguins also have the amazing ability to swim in icy cold waters to depths of up to 480 m. The kittiwake is one of many types of seabird that live on remote and exposed coastal cliffs. These seabirds have the remarkable ability to build nests from compacted seaweed and attach them to sheer rock faces with mud.

Some of the most unusual creatures that have ever been discovered live in the deep sea. The oceans can be as deep as 11 km in places, a distance that is greater in magnitude than the highest mountains. 'Deep sea' is considered to exist at depths of more than about one kilometre. At these depths there is virtually total darkness because the sun's rays do not reach that far. The temperature is also very cold because water does not conduct heat very well from the warmer water near the surface of the sea. Another physical problem is that the water pressure increases as the water depth increases. At a depth of one kilometre, the water pressure is so immense that it can be enough to crush a submarine. Another problem with the deep sea is that there is very little food. Since there is no sunlight, no plants can live in the deep sea and the only food available is that which falls from higher levels and the creatures that live in the deep sea.

Considering the harshness of the deep-sea environment, it is astounding that there is actually life even here. From the limited studies that have been carried out, it is now known that there are many creatures that live at great depths, including the viper fish, gulper eel, tripod fish, spiny eel, rat tail, snipe eel, lantern fish, dragon fish and deep-sea angler fish. These creatures have special design features to live at these depths such as strong bodies, luminescence and special sensors for navigating in the dark. Lantern fish even flash their lights on and off! It is very difficult for evolution to explain how deep-sea creatures could have evolved and what selective pressures could have brought them into such deep water. The evolutionist believes that deep-sea fish originated from ordinary fish which gradually descended down from shallow waters and then evolved the necessary features to live in the depths. However, the seas have such a stable climate and enable such freedom of movement that it is difficult to see why a fish would need to descend into the depths to survive.

In recent years it has been found that there are many tiny microbes living in some very extreme environments that were previously thought absolutely inhospitable such as live volcanic craters, the Antarctic and boiling mud. These microbes have been appropriately called 'extremophiles' and they can tolerate extreme levels of temperature, pressure, dryness, acidity and salinity. One example, called *Sulfolobus solfataricus* can survive near sulfurous volcanic vents where the temperature may be 88°C. Another extremophile, *Ferroplasma acidarmanus* can survive harsh toxic chemicals such as sulfuric acid, arsenic and cadmium. The existence of living organisms in extreme and harsh environments is very difficult to explain by evolution. However, it is just what would be expected from a Creator.

8.9 Extreme number of species

The number of different species in the natural world also gives evidence of design because it is so vast. There are an estimated 10 to 100 million different species of organism in the earth, including plants, creatures and micro-organisms. Only a small minority of these organisms have been studied or named by scientists. There are around 4,000 species of mammal, 9,000 species of bird, 20,000 species of fish, over a million species of insect and over 400,000 species of plant. Within the insect class alone there are 350,000 described species of beetle and it is estimated that there are actually over a million species in existence[5] with each species having its own unique design.

Virtually every class of creature contains species with a great variety of shapes and features that range from fat to thin, tall to short, long legs to short legs and delicate features to crude features. Even within each individual species there is tremendous variation in appearance due to the genetic potential of gene variation. Even a lifelong study could explore only a tiny fraction of features in the creatures of the natural world. Such an extreme number of different organisms gives evidence of deliberate design!

8.10 Extreme range of sizes

Examples of the great range in the weight of adult creatures and plants are shown in Table 8–1. The table shows that in the case of mammals, the blue whale is 80 million times heavier than the tiny bumblebee bat. Whereas the blue whale grows to 30 m in length, the bumblebee bat reaches only 15 cm. Flying birds also have a great range with the kori bustard weighing 18 kg which is 11,000 times greater than the bee hummingbird. Fish have the biggest range of size amongst creatures with the whale shark weighing an incredible 8,000 million times more than the dwarf pygmy gobi. Whereas the whale shark reaches 18 m in length, the dwarf pygmy gobi reaches only 2 cm!

Insects also have an astounding range of size with the Goliath beetle weighing 3,000 million times more than the fairy fly! Whereas the Goliath beetle grows to 11 cm in length, the fairy fly grows to just 0.02 mm which is so small that a microscope is needed for human observation. Plants also have a vast range of size with the sequoia tree weighing 2000 tonnes, which is 20,000 million times greater than the dwarf snow willow tree! The great range of weights and sizes in creatures provides evidence of design because it is so vast. There is hardly a class of creature or plant that does not come in an incredible range of sizes.

Table 8–1 Range in adult weight of creatures and plants

CLASS	LARGEST	SMALLEST
Mammal	120 tonnes (blue whale)	1.5 g (bumblebee bat)
Flying bird	18 kg (kori bustard)	1.6 g (bee hummingbird)
Fish	40 tonnes (whale shark)	5 mg (dwarf pygmy gobi)
Insect	100 g (Goliath beetle)	30 billionths of 1 g (fairy fly)
Tree	2000 tonnes (sequoia tree)	100 mg (dwarf snow willow)

8.11 The goodness of God in creation

As with beauty and similarity, the provision of diversity reveals God's attribute of goodness. This is because God has deliberately created creatures for every part of the earth for the good of mankind. Wherever people live and travel they will see God's handiwork. There are creatures on every type of dry land including the Arctic, Antarctic, mountains and deserts. There are also creatures in every part of the sea including the deep sea. God has even designed dolphins and other creatures to come to the surface of the sea so that it is possible to see His handiwork there. There are also creatures that live in the sky and some creatures, such as geese and vultures, that fly at great altitudes. Even when people dig deep into the earth there is usually some form of microbial life to be found! The witness of creation is also there whenever people go about their business. At every time of the day there is some kind of creature that is active. Even in the darkness of night there are many sounds to be heard from the nocturnal animal kingdom. The fullness of creation is a blessing to mankind because it provides food and materials for man and helps to reveal the attributes of the Creator.

It is ironic that there are many scientists who see the diversity of life as an evidence of evolution when it is actually an evidence of the infinite goodness of God. The diversity in the natural world also reveals the wisdom of God. The puritan writer Thomas Watson wrote this about the witness of creation:

The world is like a curious piece of tapestry, in which we may see the skill and wisdom of him that made it.[6]

Each one of the many different types of creatures and plants in nature provides evidence of the infinite skill and wisdom of God. Such evidence is encouraging because it shows how God cares about the smallest details of human life and how He cares about every part of the earth. The psalmist aptly described the great diversity of life that God has made: 'O Lord, how manifold are Your works! In wisdom You have made them all. The earth is full of Your possessions—this great and wide sea, in which are innumerable teeming things, living things both small and great.' (Psalm 104:24–25).

Modern discoveries of life on earth have demonstrated the profound truth of these verses.

Notes on Chapter 8

1 **Wilson, E.O.,** *The Diversity of life,* Penguin, 1992.

2 **Harrington, P.,** 'Nature's Helicopters', *The Magazine,* Rolls Royce, Issue 74, p. 16, September 1997.

3 **Margulis, L. and Schwartz, K.,** *Five kingdoms: an illustrated guide to the phyla of life on earth,* 3rd edition, Freeman, New York, p. 404, 1998.

4 **Daily Telegraph,** *Turtle Highway,* p. 9, March 13th 1998.

5 **Chadwick, D.H.,** 'Planet of the Beetles', *National Geographic,* Vol. 193, No. 3, pp. 100–119, 1998.

6 **Watson, T.,** *A body of divinity* (1692), The Banner of Truth Trust, Chapter 14 'The Creation', p. 116, 1965.

Man-centred features

And God said, 'See, I have given you every herb that yields seed which is on the face of all the earth, and every tree whose fruit yields seed; to you it shall be for food' (Genesis 1:29).

The first chapter of the book of Genesis teaches that plants and trees were specifically designed to produce food for man. In fact, the Bible teaches that the whole creation has been designed for man and that man has been made steward over creation. Modern discoveries have demonstrated the wonderful truth of this biblical teaching. Even though there has been a Fall and this has produced undesirable effects like weeds and pests, it is still very evident that the earth has been designed for the needs of man. This chapter gives some important examples of man-centred features in different parts of creation.

The existence of man-centred features does not necessarily provide much direct evidence against evolution. Evolutionists will always say that the features of the earth had to be just right, otherwise man would not be here to consider the question. However, this does not mean that man-centred features is an unimportant argument. Man-centred features is a type of evidence that provides positive and direct evidence for a Creator. Indeed, the Design Argument is ultimately about positive evidence for design rather than evidence against evolution. Another reason for considering man-centred features is that they show something of man's relationship with the Creator. When God created every single detail of creation, He had in mind the needs of man. It is so easy to become influenced by the thinking of the modern atheistic world that it is just due to chance that the food, materials and other parts of creation are well suited to man. In reality, it is God's providence and planning that has caused the earth to be supremely well designed for man. The study of how well the earth is designed for man can be very encouraging because it shows God's fatherly love for man.

9.1 Hallmark of design: man-centred features

Human designers put much effort into designing man-centred features in devices for human use. In Europe, the practice of designing man-centred features is called *Ergonomics* and in the USA the practice is called *Human Factors*. The design of man-centred features is so important in engineering design that there are national standards on how products should be ergonomically designed for human use.[1] The motor car is an example that shows the importance of ergonomics. A car is designed not just to survive its environment but also to provide high levels of comfort and safety for the driver. Ergonomic features in cars include seat shape, door handle shape, air conditioning and location of mirrors. If a car was designed only to survive its environment, it would not be man-centred at all and would be of little use. The man-centred features in man-made devices show that a designer was responsible for the design. In a similar way, the man-centred features in plants, creatures and other things in the earth, give evidence of deliberate design.

9.2 Man-centred food

He causes the grass to grow for the cattle, and vegetation for the service of man, that he may bring forth food from the earth (Psalm 104:14).

The Bible teaches that vegetation (Psalm 104:14) and fruit (Genesis 1:29) have been made to be of service to man. Natural foods like fruit provide important evidence for a Creator because they are often so well designed for man. Food which is ideal for human use must have several finely tuned characteristics. For example, it should have nutrients such as protein, fat, carbohydrates and vitamins. Fibre is also required in the diet to help the whole digestive process. Human food should also have the right shape and consistency to be bitten or swallowed. Convenient packaging and abundance of supply are also important. To fulfil most or all of these requirements is a very demanding task. The difficulty of producing man-centred food is demonstrated by the fact that millions of pounds go into the design of man-made food by the food industry.

Despite the wide-ranging requirements of ideal food, there are many examples of supremely well designed foods in plants and animals. Of course, farmers and scientists have used breeding techniques to optimise the characteristics of plants and animals for the needs of man. However, this does not mean that there were previously any problems with such foods. Even before selective breeding was carried out, plants and animals were well designed for man. The fact that plants and animals have the potential to be finely tuned for man only adds to the evidence for design. The following sections describe how fruit, rice and farm produce provide some fascinating examples of man-centred foods.

I FRUIT

Fig. 9–1 shows some of the fruits that are very convenient for human use. Bananas are one of the world's most highly produced crops and are very important to the economies of some countries. There are several reasons why the banana is well designed for human use. The banana is nutritious, containing carbohydrate, vitamins and roughage. The shape and size of the banana make it very convenient for biting and holding with the hand.

Fig. 9–1 Fruit with man-centred features

The consistency of the banana is just soft enough to be easy to bite but also just firm enough that the banana does not collapse when held or when a bite is taken. Even the curved shape of the banana is convenient because it means that the hand can be placed below the mouth and not in front, thus allowing the eater to see ahead! The skin of the banana has convenient crease lines so that it can be easily pulled apart in sections. The banana skin also provides a very effective protective wrapping to aid transport and storage. The banana skin even gives an indication of the freshness of the contents!

The orange is another good example of a fruit with ideal man-centred features. Like the banana, it has a nutritional content, size, shape and packaging that are convenient for man. Another very useful feature of the orange is that it has a segmented and cellular structure which is efficient at retaining juice. If the orange were just a bag of juice, then opening an orange could produce very messy results! However, the separate segments do not leak when the orange peel is removed. Even when an individual segment is broken, the cellular structure prevents any significant leakage.

The apple also has a clever and convenient method of storing liquid. Even though the contents of the apple are almost entirely juice, the apple hardly leaks at all when a bite is taken. The reason for this is that the liquid is held in tiny cells that are distributed throughout the apple and, when a bite is taken, there is no significant leakage. Human designers put great efforts into preventing leaks from cartons of fruit juice, yet the orange and apple already have a very clever solution to this problem!

II RICE

Rice is one of the most important crops in the world and it is eaten by around half of the world's population. Rice is a remarkable plant which can be turned into several kinds of food. In its most common form it is boiled and eaten as rice. However, it can also be ground to make flour, fermented to make wine and it can be processed to make rice cereals. Rice also has many uses other than as food for human consumption. The straw from the rice plant can be used to feed cattle. Rice straw can also be twisted into sticks to make fuel, plaited to make rope, mixed with clay to make bricks, used to make paper and used to make shoes. The bran from the rice grain contains oils that can be extracted and used to make soaps and cosmetics. The husks (or shells) from the grains can be used as a packaging material and for insulation. The husks can also be used as a fuel.

III FARM PRODUCE

Farm animals produce many foods which contain man-centred features. It is interesting to note that cattle were originally created as cattle (Genesis 1:24–25). This indicates that some animals were deliberately created as domesticated farm animals and that man did not have to convert wild animals into farm animals. The dairy cow is an amazingly productive food factory that produces typically 12 litres (21 pints) of milk a day which is much more than that required to feed a young calf. Some breeds of dairy cow can produce even more than 12 litres a day. The fact that there are so many animals, like horses and sheep, that produce a relatively small amount of milk through small teats strongly indicates that the cow has been deliberately designed to supply large amounts of milk for human use. There are even varieties of cow that produce different grades of creamy milk! Milk can also be used to make other dairy products like butter, cheese and yoghurts.

One of the most highly produced animal products in the world is the hen's egg. The egg is a very nutritious and versatile food indeed. Eggs can be used as the main ingredient of meals and sandwiches. However, eggs are often an important ingredient of other products such as cakes. Not only is the hen's egg nutritious, but it also comes with its own hard package which enables it to be cooked and transported in a convenient way.

9.3 Man-centred clothing materials

Then Pharaoh took his signet ring off his hand and put it on Joseph's hand; and he clothed him in garments of fine linen (Genesis 41:42).

Materials that are well suited for human clothing must have many details of design that are right, including thermal insulation, breathing properties (not airtight), comfortable texture, lightness, strength and ease of processing. These requirements are so sophisticated that extensive research goes into producing synthetic clothing materials such as nylon and lycra. Even after much research, however, natural materials such as wool and cotton are often found to provide the highest quality and comfort. Recent studies by scientists have shown that natural materials have some outstanding physical properties that make them extremely well suited for human clothing.

I WOOL

One of the best examples of a clothing material with man-centred features is sheep's wool. Historical records show that wool has played a very important role in human life for thousands of years. Unlike other animals, a sheep grows its hair very rapidly at a rate of typically two or three inches per year, which means that it can be shorn annually and produce an abundant supply. There are different sheep and goats that give different qualities of wool. For instance, the Cashmere goat produces particularly fine wool for very high quality clothing. Wool is very convenient to handle because when twisted it can be turned into yarn and rolled up for easy storage.

Wool is not only abundant and easy to store, but it has extraordinary physical properties that make it an ideal material for clothing. Wool is a good insulator because air gets trapped in the wool fibres. This means that clothing made from wool can be very lightweight. The insulating properties of wool mean that it can be used to keep things warm or cold. This is why wool is used for insulation in both cold and hot countries. Another important property of wool is that it is both porous and permeable. This means that wool can absorb perspiration and then release it slowly through evaporation. In the winter this reduces chills and in the summer it keeps the body feeling cool. Incredibly, wool even has the ability to warm up when it gets wet and this is a property that has been appreciated by shepherds over many years! A single gram of wool gives off 27 calories of heat when it goes from dry to wet.[2] Another important property of wool is that it is highly absorbent. In fact, wool is the most hydrophilic (water-loving) of all natural fibres, and is able to absorb a quantity of water equivalent to 30 percent of its own weight without feeling wet to the touch. In contrast, the figure for man-made fibres like polyester is less than 5 percent. Wool is so good at absorbing water that in biblical times, wool fleeces were left out overnight in the desert to collect water (Judges 6:38).

II COTTON
Another important clothing material is cotton. Cotton has a cool and soft feel and this makes it particularly suitable for shirts and clothes that are worn next to the skin. Like wool, cotton can be easily turned into thread and, like wool, cotton can absorb much more moisture than man-made materials. Compared to a man-made material like polyester, cotton feels relatively cool and is less likely to cause sweating. Like wool, cotton is very easy to harvest because it simply grows on plants.

III LEATHER
The leather from cowhide is also a very useful material for clothes. The toughness of leather makes it particularly suitable for high quality footwear. Like wool and cotton, leather has the very desirable property of allowing ventilation. Whereas synthetic materials can make feet sweat a lot, leather can keep feet relatively dry.

EVIDENCE OF DESIGN
Another interesting property of wool, cotton and leather is that they occur mostly in a near white colour. This is very convenient because it makes it possible to turn these materials into virtually any colour by simply adding a dye. It is very difficult for the evolutionist to explain how plants and animals are able to provide mankind with such convenient and useful materials. There is an abundant supply of natural materials that are able to satisfy all the needs of mankind for clothing. The outstanding quality and comfort of these materials is not accidental but is the result of deliberate design.

9.4 Man-centred transport
Have you given the horse strength? Have you clothed his neck with thunder (Job 39:19)?

In the present industrial era, people rely heavily on various types of transport including cars and bicycles. However, for thousands of years such means of transport were unavailable and people relied entirely on natural means of transportation, especially animal transportation. In particular, the horse has been used extensively down through the ages by people throughout the world.

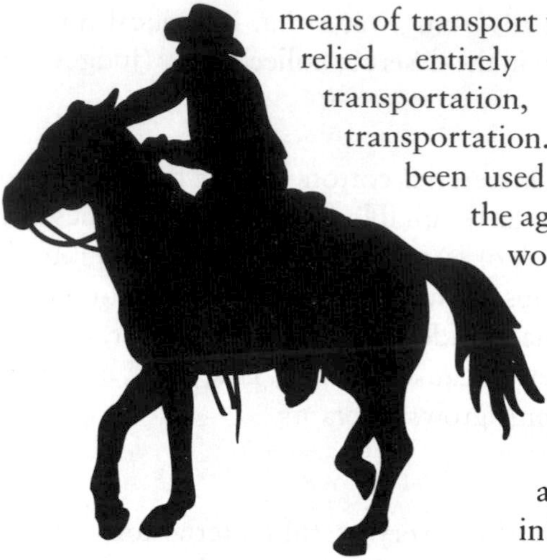

The horse is an ideal means of transport for people for the following reasons. Firstly, the shape and size of the horse's back is ideal for a person to sit on, as shown in Fig. 9–2. Secondly, the horse is just small enough for a human to climb up on. Thirdly, the horse is just big enough to find a person easy to carry. Fourthly, the horse is ideally designed for speed with a lean body and strong legs. Fifthly, the horse is able to cover large distances in one day. Sixthly, the horse can reproduce itself. Seventhly, horses come in a range of types and sizes so that a particular combination of speed, range and strength can be selected. Eighthly, the horse is completely environmentally safe. There is even a special version of a horse for dry sandy places called a camel!

Fig. 9–2 The horse: an animal with man-centred features

The horse is an outstanding example of an animal with man-centred features that has served mankind extremely well since the beginning of creation. A cow is clearly designed to produce milk, a sheep is clearly designed to produce wool and a horse is clearly designed for transportation. The fact that people have always had horses for their use is no accident but evidence of deliberate design!

9.5 Man-centred mechanical power

…much increase comes by the strength of an ox (Proverbs 14:4).

Mechanical power makes an important contribution to the well-being and standard of living of modern people. For example, the amount of earth that a mechanical digger can move in one hour would take a man many weeks to move using just a shovel. However, for thousands of years such mechanical aids were not available and people were heavily reliant on natural forms of power such as that produced by large animals. Animals like the ox, horse and elephant have provided people with a very convenient source of power for farming and building down through the ages. These animals are extremely powerful and well capable of tasks such as ploughing and carrying. The elephant can even pick large objects off the ground with its trunk.

A large effort goes into repairing and maintaining mechanical diggers because their tasks are so arduous that they suffer from much wear and tear. In contrast, animals like the ox are very reliable! The existence of powerful animals is no accident but evidence of design.

9.6 Man-centred grass

He causes the grass to grow for the cattle (Psalm 104:14).

There are a wide variety of grasses that can be used in many ways. Grass is a very durable and beautiful surface for gardens with different types of grass for dry areas and shady areas. Grass is also a superb plant for all kinds of sporting surfaces from tough rugby fields to fine putting greens. The excellent quality of grass has been demonstrated in recent years in the experimental use of artificial grass surfaces. Football clubs have found that artificial surfaces produce the wrong bounce, lead to nasty grazes for players and look unsightly. Of course, grass is also very useful for animal grazing. How well grass is designed!

9.7 Man-centred materials

And the king commanded them to quarry large stones, costly stones, and hewn stones, to lay the foundation of the temple. So Solomon's builders, Hiram's builders, and the Gebalites quarried them; and they prepared timber and stones to build the temple (1 Kings 5:17–18).

Natural materials have always been important for the making of buildings and tools. Before the industrial era, mankind relied completely on the materials of wood, metals and stone. Even today, many industrial and building materials come straight from the natural world. Probably the most useful and convenient material is wood because it is both very strong and very attractive. Wood has such a good strength to weight ratio that it is still used occasionally in aircraft manufacture. Bamboo, a type of grass, is another superb structural material that has an in-built efficient structural shape. Bamboo consists of a hollow tubular structure that makes it extremely light. It is very suitable for scaffolding and frameworks for buildings and is still used extensively for these applications in many parts of the world. Mankind has always had a constant local supply of wood because trees grow continuously throughout the world. Of course, if forests and trees are not carefully preserved, then shortages arise. However, with careful stewardship there will always be an ample supply of wood.

Metals also provide a very useful set of materials for mankind. There is a whole range of metals including copper, tin, lead, zinc, aluminium, iron, magnesium, titanium, silver and gold. The range of metals is such that there are materials to satisfy virtually every need of mankind. Metals like copper and aluminium are excellent for electric wires and cooking utensils because of their good conducting properties. Iron is a very strong material that is ideal for casting. The metals listed above can also be combined to make many thousands of varied materials that have their own unique properties. One of the most important combinations is that of iron and carbon to make steel. Steel is not only very strong but it also has a very special structure that can be made hard by heat treatment. Copper is often combined with tin to make bronze which is a very useful bearing material.

The great variety of materials in the earth gives modern man a selection of approximately 80,000 different types of material to choose from.[3] It is easy to take woods and metals for granted but the fact is that they have been wonderfully designed and supplied for the use of mankind. It is also significant that the most useful materials are also the most abundant in the earth. For example, iron and aluminium are much more abundant than tungsten and titanium and are also of much more use. The variety, usefulness and appropriate abundance of materials in the earth gives great evidence of design.

Creatures have also provided mankind with important tools and materials throughout the history of the world. For example, bird feathers have provided an abundant supply of high quality 'quill' pens, their stiff hollow shafts being ideal for storing ink. Feathers have also been used to guide arrows, whilst bird bones have been used for tools and needles. Down feathers are still widely used today to fill pillows and duvets with a soft insulating material.

9.8 Man-centred fuel

Now the servants and officers who had made a fire of coals stood there, for it was cold, and they warmed themselves (John 18:18).

Energy has always been important for heating, cooking and manufacturing. In modern times, fuel is also very useful for transportation. Ideally, fuel should have the following properties: very high energy density (energy per unit weight), ease of ignition, abundance and local availability. This is exactly what is found in nature. For example, wood contains a great amount of energy and a large log can burn for many hours. Before the industrial era, wood was an abundant material that was always locally available. Wood is even convenient to light because ignition can be achieved by rubbing together two small twigs.

At this point it can be noted just how incredibly useful wood is in so many different ways. During its lifetime, a tree performs many important functions such as producing oxygen, providing a home for animals and birds, collecting dust from the air, producing fruit, providing shade and providing beauty. It can then be chopped up to provide very useful materials for housing and furniture. It can then be burnt to provide vital fuel. Finally, the ashes can have uses such as a fertiliser! The value of wood to mankind has been priceless. Trees are truly a marvel that have served and still serve man extremely well.

In modern times, coal, oil and gas are some of the main fuels that supply the energy needs of industry. The reason for this is that they have a truly amazing energy density level. The energy contained in oil is so great that a car, weighing a tonne, can be driven several hundred miles on just 20 litres of fuel.

9.9 Man-centred clocks, calendars and navigation

Then God said, 'Let there be lights in the firmament of the heavens to divide the day from the night; and let them be for signs and seasons, and for days and years' (Genesis 1:14).

Clocks, calendars and navigational aids have always played a very important part in human life. In the modern world people rely on clocks and calendars to help them keep appointments. People also rely on compasses and satellites for navigation, particularly with air and sea travel. However, for thousands of years there were no clocks or compasses and people had to rely completely on natural systems like the sun, moon and stars. These systems provided and still provide a convenient means for knowing the time and for enabling a system of navigation. The sun, for example, can be used to calculate the time of day using a sundial. The sundial makes a shadow on a clock template and can give time very accurately. When there are separate templates for each month of the year, the time can be determined to within a few minutes of the correct time.

The moon is a useful calendar because its shape in the sky goes through a predictable monthly cycle. In the northern hemisphere, when the moon is waxing (increasing illumination) the illumination forms on one side to make the letter D, whereas when the moon is waning (decreasing illumination) the illumination forms on the other side to make the letter C. If a month is assumed to start with a new moon, then the first quarter ends when the moon is a half moon in the shape of a D, the second quarter ends when there is a full moon and the third quarter ends when there is a half moon in the shape of C. Since the moon cycle has a total period of 29.5 days, the lunar phases of 1st, 2nd, 3rd and 4th quarter last approximately a week each which is a convenient time period. In fact, with practice, the exact day of the month can be determined by analysing the size and shape of the moon. It is amazing that whilst the moon has an important function of producing the tidal effect, it also performs the function of a calendar system!

The stars also have a very important function as a navigation system for mankind. They are ideally suited to navigation because they form very distinctive patterns in the night-time sky. In fact, stars are very well designed for several reasons. Firstly, they are ideal for navigation. Secondly, they provide a little light for night-time creatures. Thirdly, they make a beautiful spectacle from the earth. The usefulness, convenience and beauty of sun, moon and stars provide great evidence of design.

9.10 The Anthropic Principle

Some evolutionists recognise that the universe has many physical properties that must be exactly right for life and intelligence to exist. The belief that the universe is finely tuned for life is sometimes called the *Anthropic Principle*. Whilst it is commendable that some evolutionists recognise that the universe is remarkably well-suited to life, it is sad that they still refuse to believe in a Creator. As with the Gaia hypothesis, the Anthropic Principle shows how many scientists will do anything to avoid the conclusion of a Creator. All man-made machines are the result of intelligent design. In the same way, the universe is the result of the deliberate design of a Creator.

9.11 The goodness and fatherly love of God in creation

The special man-centred features in the natural world not only give evidence of deliberate design but they also reveal God's attributes of goodness and fatherly love. It is wonderful to think that the horse was specially designed to give human beings a convenient ride! The evolutionist believes that it is a pure coincidence that animals and plants are so suitable for the use of mankind. The sad consequence of this belief is that people either disbelieve in God or believe that God is very remote and uncaring. The reality is that the whole of creation has been wonderfully designed for mankind and this shows God's wonderful grace towards all people. This is why the psalmist said: 'The Lord is good to all, and His tender mercies are over all His works' (Psalm 145:9).

Notes on Chapter 9

1 **Pheasant, S.,** *Ergonomics*, British Standards Institute, 1987.

2 **Hyde, N.,** 'Wool: fabric of history', *National Geographic,* 173(5), pp. 552–591, 1988.

3 **Ashby, M.F.,** *Materials selection in mechanical design*, Pergamon Press, p. 4, 1992.

The unique design of man

For You formed my inward parts; You covered me in my mother's womb. I will praise You, for I am fearfully and wonderfully made; marvellous are Your works, and that my soul knows very well (Psalm 139:13-14).

Humans have many unique characteristics that make them very different from animals. In addition, humans have abilities that far exceed those required for survival. This chapter describes how the human being has a unique design in body, mind and spirit. The unique design of the human being gives great evidence for a Creator.

There are ten particular characteristics of the human being that are unique:
- Upright stature
- Skilful hands
- Unique skin
- Intricate language
- Intricate facial expressions
- Unique intellect
- Unique genetic code
- Unique reproduction
- Spiritual being
- Delicate beauty

This chapter describes a total of 30 unique features of the human being which create the unique characteristics described above. The characteristic of delicate beauty is dealt with in the next chapter.

10.1 Upright stature

Man is the only creature with arms that can move with an upright stature. In technical terms, a human is a 'biped' (two-legged) whereas other land creatures are generally quadrupeds (four-legged). The skeletons of an ape and a human are shown in Fig. 10–1 to illustrate how a human is designed

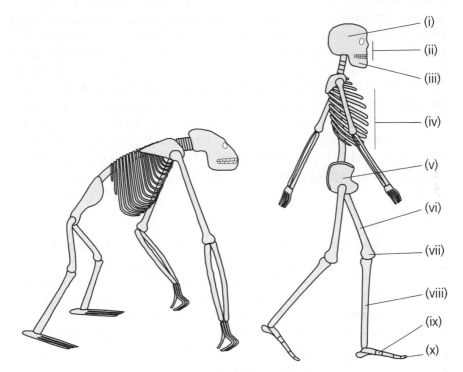

(a) Ape　　　　　　　　　　　　**(b)** Human

KEY

(i)	Fine balance	(vi)	Angled femur bones
(ii)	Flat face	(vii)	Fully extendable knees
(iii)	Upright skull	(viii)	Long legs
(iv)	Straight back	(ix)	Arched feet
(v)	Fully extendable hips	(x)	Strong big toes

Fig. 10–1 Unique structural features that are required for an upright posture

for bipedal motion and an ape is designed for quadrupedal motion. Even though many birds can walk upright, they have limited capabilities on land because they have no arms. To be able to stand upright, the human being has at least ten unique structural features which are summarised in Fig. 10–1. There are so many unique features required for bipedal motion that it is impossible for a quadruped to gradually evolve into a biped. Evolutionists have often claimed to have found intermediate extinct creatures between man and apes. However, in every case, the creature is either fully bipedal or fully quadrupedal, showing that it is actually either fully human or fully ape. Evolutionists have totally failed to show how a quadruped could evolve into a biped. The unique structural features required for an upright stature are discussed briefly in the following sections.

I FINE BALANCE

Standing and moving on two legs requires a finer sense of balance than the quadrupedal motion of apes. Humans mainly achieve balance through sensors in the inner ear. The inner ear has a network of intricate fluid-filled canals which contain sensors which are sensitive to movement and gravity. The sensors consist of fine hairs which send out signals to indicate the direction and speed of head movements. The canals are arranged in three planes which are at right-angles to each other in order to give three-dimensional sensing. Humans have a much more complex design of inner ear than apes.

II FLAT FACE

Humans have a flat face so that the eyes have a field of view which extends down to the ground in front of the feet. The ability to see the ground just in front of the feet is important for humans because the problem of tripping is greater for bipedal motion than for quadrupedal motion.

III UPRIGHT SKULL

The position at which the spinal cord enters the skull is called the 'foramen magnum'. In the case of humans, the foramen magnum is located at the bottom of the skull, as shown in Fig. 10–1. This means that the most natural position for the head is looking forward in the upright position. If humans attempt to walk on all four limbs, the head has to be forced up in order to look ahead. When babies crawl on four limbs, it can be observed that they have to make a big effort in order to hold their head up for looking ahead. In contrast to humans, apes have a foramen magnum located at the back of the skull so that the most natural position for the head is looking forward in the horizontal position. Even though an ape can look forward when sitting upright, this is only possible because his head is bent downwards.

IV STRAIGHT BACK
The straight back of humans is ideal for an upright stature because the torso and head are directly above the hips in the standing position. In contrast, apes have a curved back and so the torso projects out in front of the hips. This means that apes must use their arms and hands to support their weight, as shown in Fig. 10–1. This is why apes are sometimes referred to as knuckle-walkers. The human spine is slightly undulating and has the shape of the letter 'S'. In contrast, the spine of apes is bent in the shape of the letter 'C'.

V FULLY EXTENDABLE HIP JOINTS
Humans have a pelvis which allows the femur bone to be fully extended for an upright posture. In contrast, the hip joints of apes cannot fully extend to the upright position.

VI ANGLED FEMUR BONES
When looking from the front, humans have femur bones which are angled inwards as they come down from the hip joints to the knees. This has the effect of making the knees close together and the feet close together. Having feet close together keeps the feet nearly under the centre of the body and this gives stability during walking and running. During walking and running, the body is only supported by one leg at any instant in time and so the body can easily topple over if the legs are not right under the body. If the feet were not close together during walking and running, then the body would be thrown from one side to the other as the body landed on each

foot. In contrast to humans, the femur bones of apes drop down vertically, making the knees relatively far apart and the feet far apart. When apes (or bears) try to walk on two legs, it can be observed that they sway awkwardly from side to side as they try to maintain balance. Apes must have widely spaced feet because this gives stability in quadrupedal motion. The angled femur bone of humans also explains why humans are so good at standing on one leg.

VII FULLY EXTENDABLE KNEE JOINTS

The human knee joint can extend fully so that the leg can be made straight and the body upright. In fact, the human knee joint also *locks* in the upright position. This feature makes standing easy because the muscles do not need to be kept in tension. In contrast, the knee joint of apes is not fully extendable and apes must always have bent legs.

VIII LONG LEGS

The length of human legs is about half the total length of the body. These long legs make it possible to walk and run very long distances with relative ease. In contrast, the legs of apes are only about a third of the length of their body. There is an interesting contrast between the limbs of humans and apes because humans have long legs and short arms whereas apes have short legs and long arms. The arms of apes must be longer than their legs because the hands must reach the ground to allow quadrupedal movement on land.

IX ARCHED FEET

The human foot is clearly designed for an upright stature. The human foot is arched between the heel and the ball of the foot and the toes are relatively small. The foot has around 26 bones and many muscles, ligaments, tendons and nerves so that the foot can flex between the heel and the ball. The arched structure of the foot makes it easy for a person to press down on the ball of the foot which is important for balance and control during standing and upright movement. For example, when standing, a person can maintain a balanced upright stature by pressing down on the ball of the foot and by adjusting the position of the upper body. The ability to press on the ball of the foot is also important for movements such as standing on tiptoe, running and turning. The arched structure of the human foot also helps to absorb shocks during walking and running. The rigidity of the foot is just right for bipedal standing and movement. The foot has enough rigidity so that standing is not a strain but it also has enough flexibility so that it can flex during walking and running. In contrast, the feet of monkeys and apes are like hands and are suited to gripping branches.

X STRONG BIG TOES

Humans have a strong big toe which is close to the other toes. This feature is important for walking and running because, for each step, the final push from the ground comes from the big toe. In order to propel the body forwards in a controlled manner, the big toe must be very strong. In contrast to humans, the big toe of apes is like a flexible thumb which is designed for gripping branches. When apes attempt to walk with an upright stature, they cannot make a firm push from their big toe.

AMAZING ABILITIES

The balance demonstrated by sportsmen such as tennis players and ice skaters can be astounding and vastly superior to any two-legged movement of animals. Professional tennis players have such controlled movement and balance that they can sprint around a court forwards, sideways and backwards and intercept a tennis ball travelling at over 100 kilometres per hour and hit the ball back over the net with great precision. Olympic ice skaters have such fine balance that they can jump in the air and spin around two times before landing with such precision that they carry on gliding gracefully across the ice. Only humans are capable of such sophisticated bipedal movement.

10.2 Skilful hands

A very important consequence of the upright stature of humans is that it enables their hands to be designed for uses other than basic living tasks. In the case of animals, all of their limbs are designed for very specific survival tasks such as locomotion, fighting and eating. Human hands are unique because they are not designed just for survival tasks but also for holding, gripping and performing delicate operations. According to evolution, human hands evolved because they were useful for holding tools for farming and hunting. However, if humans had evolved only enough to become farmers and hunters, then there would not be a need for great dexterity of the hands. The fact that many farming and hunting tasks can be carried out with thick gloves shows that micro-fine control is not necessarily required for survival.

I HIGHLY DEXTEROUS HANDS

Researchers have estimated that the human hand is capable of 58 distinct and precise movements. One of the reasons why human hands are so dexterous is that there are many intricate joints and muscles in the hand and forearm. There are around 27 separate bones in the hand which are joined together by a great number of ligaments. There are also around 35 muscles which control the movement of the hand. 18 of these muscles are in the forearm and 17 are in the palm of the hand. Forces are transmitted to the fingers by a network of tendons. The strength and agility of the hands is such that humans can perform astounding levels of controlled movement. Apes and monkeys have a relatively simple design of hand and they do not have the fine control that humans have.

II OPPOSABLE THUMBS

Another unique feature of the human hand is that it has fully 'opposable' thumbs which can make face-to-face contact with the end of each finger. Human thumbs are opposable for two main reasons. Firstly, the human thumb is relatively very long. Secondly, the palm of the hand is very flexible so that the thumb can be bent round to meet the tips of any of the four fingers. There are two main types of grip. One type is the 'pinch grip' where the thumb pinches the tip of one of the fingers. This type of grip is used to hold a pen or a small object with great precision. The other type of grip is a 'power grip' where the whole hand grasps a bar. When gripping a sports racket, the four fingers are placed on one side of the racket and the thumb is placed on the other side to make a very strong and firm grip. Even though apes can make their thumbs touch the palms of their hands, the thumbs cannot make a pinch grip with the fingers. Sir Isaac Newton said that the thumb alone would be enough to convince him of the existence of a Creator. The uniqueness of the human thumb does indeed clearly point to a Creator.

III LARGE CONTROL CENTRE FOR HANDS

The part of the brain responsible for muscular movements in the body is called the motor cortex. About a quarter of the entire motor cortex is devoted to controlling the muscles of the hands even though the hands are a relatively small part of the body. No other creatures have such a relatively large section of the brain dedicated to controlling hands.

AMAZING ABILITIES

The great strength and agility of the human hands enables humans to perform amazing feats in activities such as writing, music, art, surgery, carpentry, engineering and sport. Music is one area where the extraordinary control of fingers can be clearly apparent. A concert pianist playing a sonata can accurately play several different notes every second for up to half an hour. Fig. 10–2 shows just one bar of music from the third movement of Beethoven's Moonlight Sonata No. 14 in C sharp minor which is played *presto agitato,* which means very fast. The pace of the music is so fast that the 27 notes in this bar are typically played in about one and a half seconds! In each split second, the pianist's fingers are placed in exactly the right place, with the right force and for the right length of time. The third movement contains about 6,500 individual notes and typically

Fig. 10–2 Extract from Beethoven's Moonlight Sonata in C sharp minor

takes about 7 minutes to perform. During the 7 minutes, the pianist plays an average of about 16 notes per second!

Such extraordinary feats in piano playing are not achievable by just a few gifted people. The potential for this level of performance is there whether the pianist is originally from a jungle tribe in Borneo or from a modern culture. In fact, almost any child who is given a thorough training in piano playing can make a very good attempt at the Moonlight Sonata by the age of 15.

The agility of the hands is also demonstrated in everyday activities such as the tying of shoelaces and the fastening of buttons. It is very difficult for evolution to explain why such incredible levels of dexterity should exist in the hands. Indeed, it is very difficult for evolution to explain how people from a jungle tribe can have the potential for playing concert-standard music when their immediate ancestors were supposedly adapted only to living in the jungle! In contrast, the capabilities of human hands are just what would be expected from a loving Creator.

10.3 Unique skin

According to the theory of evolution, the human being should have a type of fur-covered skin that does not need protecting out-of-doors because this would give a survival advantage especially during cold winters. The theory of evolution would also predict that the skin should be thick and tough because this would make it resistant to cuts and grazes. However, what we actually find is that all human beings are naked and must wear clothes for protection against the weather. In addition, human skin is very fine and easily cut and humans must wear protective clothing when carrying out many physical activities. There is no doubt that human skin is deliberately designed for beauty and sensitivity.

I FINE TEMPERATURE CONTROL

One important function of fine skin is that it helps a person to maintain a comfortable body temperature. In the case of animals, they have a permanent layer of thick insulation and therefore they can get uncomfortably hot after exerting themselves or when the environment is hot. Animals can also get uncomfortably cold because when the temperature is low they cannot put on extra insulation. However, in the case of humans, there is much better temperature regulation because of the properties of skin. Skin allows the body to cool down quickly because skin is very thin and because skin releases heat through vaporisation and sweating. Vaporisation occurs continually as water from the body condenses into water vapour. Sweating only occurs when a person gets very hot. The most important reason why humans can regulate temperature is that they can adjust their clothing. In the vast majority of climates, humans need to wear clothing to keep warm when at rest. When humans get hot through vigorous activity, they can take clothes off to allow heat to escape from the body. In cold weather, humans can put on many layers of clothes to keep warm.

II FINE SENSE OF TOUCH

Another important function of fine skin is to provide a very fine sense of touch. There are two main types of sensors in the skin which give feedback about the nature of contact: tactile sensors and temperature sensors. Tactile sensors consist of a nerve ending inside a fluid-filled capsule and these detect touch and pressure. Tactile sensors are sometimes called mechano-receptors. Temperature sensors consist of free nerve endings and there are separate sensors for detecting cold and heat. Temperature sensors are sometimes called thermo-receptors. There are many thousands of sensors throughout the body so that the skin can detect contact on any part of the body. When an object comes into contact with human skin, the pressure of contact and the temperature of the object are detected by the sensors in the skin and the information is sent to the brain for analysis. The skin is so sensitive that the brain can often work out what object is touching the skin before the eyes are used to look at the object. One very useful and important application of fine touch is in human surgery. Trained surgeons have a remarkable sense of touch in their fingertips which enables them to control force and position in surgical procedures with great precision. The hands and fingers have a particularly high density of sensors with many thousands of separate sensors in each hand. Another feature of the hand, which improves the sensitivity of touch, is the complete lack of hair on the palms of the hands and the underside of the fingers.

III UNIQUE EYEBROWS

The fine skin of humans means that perspiration can run down the forehead towards the eyes. However, eyebrows keep perspiration out of the eyes by providing a barrier that can soak up or redirect water. It is very difficult to imagine how evolution could produce eyebrows because they perform a relatively *minor* function rather than a vital function. According to evolution, people who accidentally developed eyebrows had a better chance of survival than people without eyebrows and therefore only people with eyebrows survived. However, such reasoning is absurd because eyebrows can hardly make the difference between surviving and not surviving! In contrast, eyebrows are just what would be expected from a Creator because a Creator would understand the convenience of having something which keeps perspiration out of the eyes.

EVIDENCE OF DESIGN

The existence of fine skin gives evidence that the Creator wants man to be comfortable, to enjoy life and also to be skilful. The ability of humans to regulate body temperature with clothes means that humans can almost always maintain a comfortable body temperature. Fine skin enables people to get pleasure from touching a variety of natural and man-made textures such as petals, wood, marble, and felt. Fine skin is very useful to blind people because they can use their sense of touch as an important means of sensing the environment. The sense of touch can be developed to such a level that it is possible to read text in the form of Braille by touch alone. The sensitivity of the skin also means that people can make intimate contact with each other. This allows two people, such as a mother and baby, to feel in close union.

10.4 Intricate language

Humans have the unique ability to communicate through complex language. There are several thousand languages in the world and each one contains thousands of words. Words are combined according to the rules of grammar of each particular language to give an infinite range of meaning. The sound-producing organ of the human being is the voice box (larynx). The voice box is located at the top of the windpipe (trachea) which is the tube between the lungs and the throat (pharynx). The voice box contains the vocal cords (vocal folds) which vibrate and produce sound waves as air passes over them.

The pitch of the sound depends on the shape of the vocal cords and the shape of the vocal tract which acts as a resonator. The vocal tract mainly consists of the windpipe, larynx, throat, mouth and nasal passages. The tongue and lips also play an important part in modifying the sound of the voice. The human voice box and vocal tract are supremely well designed to produce a range of clear and complex sounds. In contrast, the voice box and vocal tract of apes and monkeys are relatively crude and they are incapable of speaking human languages. There are at least four unique features to the human voice mechanism.

I UNIQUE SHAPE OF VOCAL TRACT

The human vocal tract has an ideal shape for producing clear sounds and a wide range of pitch. Apes have a very different shape of vocal tract and can only produce crude sounds. One of the unique features of the human vocal tract is that the voice box is located low down in the throat. This low position allows the tongue a greater range of positions to produce a greater range of vowel sounds. In contrast, other animals such as apes and monkeys have a voice box located high up and they cannot produce precise vowel sounds. The internal dome shape of the human mouth is also thought to be acoustically beneficial.

II FINE CONTROL OF VOCAL TRACT

Humans have fine muscular control over the shape of the vocal cords and vocal tract so that it is possible to control pitch and volume very precisely. There are an estimated 100 muscles involved in controlling the shape of the human vocal cords and vocal tract. In contrast, apes have far fewer muscles.

III UNIQUE TONGUE AND LIPS

Humans have fine control over the tongue for producing precise sounds including all the vowel sounds. The tongue also helps to shape many consonant sounds. Finely controlled lips also play an important part in producing precisely controlled sounds in humans. For example, 'p' and 'b' sounds are made when pressure, which is built up in the mouth, is released suddenly. 'p' is unvoiced and 'b' is voiced. The 'm' sound is made by releasing air down the nose whilst holding the mouth closed to give a 'cul-de-sac' resonator in the mouth. Consonant sounds like 'l' and 'd' are made by tongue movements. There are about one hundred different sounds that humans use in speech. These sounds are combined in very intricate ways to produce thousands of different words. In addition, intonation and accent are used to produce particular meanings in language. Apes do not have fine control over the lips and tongue and can only produce a limited range of sounds.

IV UNIQUE LANGUAGE CENTRE IN BRAIN

The human brain has areas dedicated to processing language and in general these are situated in the left cerebral hemisphere. When listening to speech, information comes from the ears to the brain where it is analysed and interpreted. When talking, the brain sends signals to the muscles in the voice box, throat, mouth, lips, tongue and chest for breathing control. The areas of the brain concerned with speaking are the Broca's area and Wernicke's area. Apes do not have areas in their brain dedicated to the processing of speech.

EVIDENCE OF DESIGN

It is easy to take for granted the complexity of human language because we can become so familiar with our own mother tongue. However, when one hears an unfamiliar foreign language, or tries to learn a foreign language, it becomes clear that language is very subtle and complicated. Whilst it is true that animals also communicate by voice, and they sometimes use frequencies outside the range of human speech, their communication abilities are very basic compared to humans. It is very difficult for evolution to explain why humans are capable of fine speech if humans have evolved simply to become farmers and hunters. It is also difficult for evolution to explain why there is no evidence of language gradually evolving over time. Languages spoken by supposedly primitive people such as stone-age man were just as complex as modern languages.

10.5 Intricate facial expressions

Humans have the unique ability to make intricate facial expressions.

I ABSENCE OF FACIAL FUR

One of the reasons why humans can make intricate facial expressions is that the face is not covered by fur. Of course, a man may have a beard, but even in this case the face is not completely covered.

II UNIQUE FACIAL MUSCLES

Another reason why humans can make facial expressions is that the face has many bones and muscles. There are about 14 bones and 53 muscles in the human face. The muscles are arranged around the eyelids, lips, nose, and external ear, and also within the cheek and scalp. There are many different types of expressions that can be made such as smiling, laughing, disapproval, confusion, grief, anger, boredom and so on. For each type of expression there are many variations. For example, there are many different types of smile and for each type there are many possible levels of intensity. Researchers have claimed that the human being can make several thousand different discernable facial expressions. Apes have relatively few facial muscles and are capable of only a handful of different facial expressions.

THE IMPORTANCE OF FACIAL EXPRESSIONS

The ability to make expressions is very important in human communication and relationships. Even though we may not be aware of it, we are constantly studying the expressions of people around us in order to anticipate the thoughts and reactions of those people. Many of our actions and questions are triggered by what we see in other people's faces. For example, when we see someone looking worried, we ask them what is wrong and when we see someone smiling, we often smile in response.

10.6 Unique intellect

The human brain is widely acknowledged as being the most complicated structure known in the universe. Human beings have a unique level of intelligence and self-awareness which is vastly greater than that required for farming and hunting. The fact that animals can survive very well by hunting and finding food with very little intelligence demonstrates that a great brain is not required for such tasks. The brain has three main sections: the large cerebrum, the cerebellum and the brain stem which is connected to the spinal cord. The cerebrum has two hemispheres called cerebral hemispheres. In general, the right hemisphere controls the left side of the body and the left hemisphere controls the right side of the body. Research has shown that specific areas of the brain are concerned with specific tasks such as speech, sight, hearing, sensory input and muscular control.

I LARGE SIZE

The human brain is much larger than the brain of apes and monkeys. The human brain has as many as 100 billion neurons and over 1,000 connections per neuron. This means that the total number of connections in the brain is about 100 trillion. This vast number of nerve cells and connections gives humans a fantastic capacity for learning and memory. It is important to note that the connections between nerve cells in the brain are not random but precisely co-ordinated so that every part of the brain is 'wired-up' correctly. For example, when sensory signals are sent to the brain they have to be sent to the right place for analysis. Also, when one area of the brain decides to take action, that area of the brain has to communicate with other appropriate areas in the brain and instructions have to be sent out to the right parts of the body. The complexity of the circuitry of the brain is beyond human comprehension and the study of the brain is an awesomely challenging task. Dr Gerald Edelman, a brain researcher at New York's Rockefeller University, summed up the challenge in this way:

Suppose I understood everything about how the brain works, I couldn't possibly visualise the process. Just to count the connections to the cortex at one per second would take 32 million years.[1]

II UNIQUE CEREBRAL CORTEX

The cerebral hemispheres are covered with a thin layer of matter a few millimetres thick called the cerebral cortex. The cerebral cortex is made of grey matter and it is here that humans have conscious thought. Beneath the cortex is the white matter. The grey matter contains the bodies of nerve cells which control brain activity. The white matter contains nerve fibres called axons and these carry information between nerve cells by conducting electrical impulses. What most distinguishes the human brain from the brain of every other creature is the relative size of the cerebral cortex. Only human beings have a very significant cerebral cortex and only in humans does it have great quantities of foldings. Such foldings maximise the surface area of the grey matter and allow a maximum amount of grey matter to be packed in the skull. Given the size of the human skull, the human brain contains an astonishing level of optimum design.

III UNIQUE CAPACITY FOR CONSCIOUS THOUGHT

Humans have the unique ability to think, have self-awareness, create and have emotional feelings. The human brain also has a unique ability to appreciate beauty. For example, whilst the left cerebral hemisphere contains areas for controlling speech, the right cerebral hemisphere contains an area for appreciating music. The theory of evolution has no explanation as to why there should be a part of the brain dedicated to appreciating music! The unique ability of humans to think is demonstrated by the very basic level of self-consciousness that animals possess. Animals have fine senses, reflexes and instincts but have no ability to think and create as humans do.

AMAZING ABILITIES

One of the most amazing abilities of the brain is to respond appropriately to the vast amount of information it receives from the sensors in the body. There are so many sensors in the body that the brain can receive millions of pieces of information per second. Out of this flood of data, some information is important and some is not. However, the brain has an ability to filter the information and to concentrate on the essential information.

Some clear examples of great intellectual achievements are found in the works of composers of classical music such as Wolfgang Amadeus Mozart (1756–1791). Composers like Mozart had a phenomenal output both in terms of the quality and quantity of their compositions. Even though

Mozart only lived until he was 35, he wrote over 600 musical compositions including over 40 symphonies. Each one of the compositions represents a beautiful masterpiece involving great musical skill and creativity. A single symphony can contain tens of thousands of notes all arranged in a very precise way. And yet Mozart was producing such sophisticated compositions at the rate of over two per month.

The musicians who play classical music also clearly demonstrate a phenomenal intellectual capacity. Each time concert pianists perform, they learn from memory a new piece of music that may have the order of 10,000 notes. For every note, there are at least three pieces of musical information that have to be remembered because each note has a pitch, length and loudness. On top of this the performer must combine the notes in such a way that there is feeling in the music. Of course, these pieces of information are not necessarily memorised individually, but they must nevertheless be 'stored' in patterns in the pianist's mind.

It is not just musicians who exhibit great intellectual capacity. Virtually every human being performs great intellectual feats such as the learning of an entire language consisting of thousands of words and complex grammar. Another incredible ability of the human brain is the ability to remember scenes that occurred decades ago.

It is very difficult for scientists to understand how the brain can perform its amazing feats, let alone begin to speculate how it could have evolved. It is very difficult for evolution to explain why the human being should need to develop such intellect and what 'selection pressures' ever existed to cause such abilities to evolve. The amazing capacity of the human brain provides powerful evidence for a Creator.

10.7 Unique genetic code

Every physical detail of the human body is specified in the human genome (complete human genetic code). The human genome is unique and distinctly different to that of every animal. Evolutionists often point out that about 98% of the genetic code of humans and chimpanzees is very similar. At first sight, this level of similarity in the genetic code might appear to show that there is very little difference between humans and chimpanzees. However, much of the genetic code is concerned with specifying biochemical details such as the structures of cells. Since all creatures have a similar biochemistry, it is not surprising that there is much similarity between the genetic code of humans and chimpanzees. The fact that there is 2% difference in the genetic code actually shows that there are significant differences between humans and chimpanzees in the overall structure of the body and mind. Indeed, this chapter describes 30 unique features of the human body and mind.

The significance of 2% difference in the genetic code is illustrated by the number of units of information (nucleotides) this represents in the DNA. Since the human genome contains the order of three billion nucleotides, 2% of the genetic code represents about sixty million units of information. Sixty million units of information is not a small genetic difference! According to evolution, there have been millions of genetic mistakes that have caused humans to evolve from monkeys or apes. However, this could not have occurred because characteristics such as upright stature cannot evolve step by step.

10.8 Unique reproduction

I UNRESTRICTED TIMING OF BIRTH

Humans have a unique characteristic of being able to conceive and give birth at any time of the year. In contrast, animals conceive and give birth at particular times of the year. In general, animals have a reproductive cycle whereby they give birth in the spring. This timing is important because it gives the offspring time to develop enough strength to survive the winter. In the case of humans, the problem of winter is not relevant because babies are sheltered indoors. The unique reproduction cycle of humans is not surprising because a husband and wife do not have physical union only to produce children. The act of physical union between and husband and wife also has the purpose of creating a bond in marriage. In contrast, animals only have physical union in order to produce offspring.

II LONG CHILDHOOD

Humans are physically very delicate at birth and need very careful protection and nurturing as babies. In contrast, the offspring of animals are generally very robust and survive in the wild with relatively little nursing. Humans also have a relatively long childhood with boys developing mentally and physically until they are typically 18 and girls developing until they are typically 16. In contrast, animals have a relatively short period of development. Indeed, animals need to develop fast so that they can survive independently in the wild from a young age. One reason for having a long childhood is that humans must learn many mental and physical skills. In the case of animals, mental learning is relatively minimal because they do not have complex language and because they can do many things through instinct such as nest-building and migration. A long childhood also enables strong family bonds to be established.

10.9 Spiritual being

The most important unique characteristic of humans is that they are spiritual beings, made in the image of God (Genesis 1:27) and capable of having fellowship with God. There is great evidence for the spiritual nature of human beings.

I UNIQUE CONSCIENCE

All people have an intrinsic sense of right and wrong showing that the law of God is written on their hearts (Romans 2:15). Even in our atheistic western society, people often refer to concepts such as justice and moral values. In addition, people have a conscience and sometimes feel a sense of guilt about their wrong actions.

II UNIQUE INTEREST IN SPIRITUAL LIFE

It is remarkable that every tribe of people, even if discovered in the remotest jungle, has some interest in spiritual life. This is not surprising because God has put eternity into the hearts of man (Ecclesiastes 3:11). Even in modern times, many people have an interest in supernatural powers and modern types of entertainment such as science fiction often have a supernatural content.

10.10 Evidence of design

Even though the human body has been affected by the Fall, it is still evident that humans are fearfully and wonderfully made. There are so many unique features in the human body that man could not have evolved by genetic mistakes. The Bible commentator Matthew Henry believed that the existence of the human body and soul was enough to demonstrate the existence of a Creator. He wrote:

The frame and structure of human bodies, and especially the most excellent powers, faculties and capacities of human souls, do abundantly prove that there is a Creator and that He is God.[2]

10.11 The purpose of man's design
It is important to realise that the unique features of the human being have important purposes.

I TO HAVE DOMINION OVER THE EARTH
The special physical features of man, such as his upright stature, agile hands and great intellectual capacity, enable humans to have complete dominion over all the creatures of the earth as God intended (Genesis 1:28 and Psalm 8:5–8). God has shown His goodness towards man by giving man such superior abilities and making it very easy for him to have dominion over the earth.

II TO REMIND US THAT WE ARE DIFFERENT
The unique features of the human being, such as his upright stature, remind humans that they are different to animals. Matthew Henry says the following about the stature of human beings:

Man has this advantage above the beasts, in the structure of his body, that whereas they are made to look downwards, as their spirits must go, he is made erect, to look upwards, because upwards his spirit must shortly go and his thoughts should now rise.[3]

III TO ENJOY PHYSICAL LIFE
The unique features of man have a purpose of enabling man to enjoy physical life. Man's fine skin enables him to maintain a comfortable body temperature and to enjoy physical contact with objects and with other human beings. Having an upright stature and agile hands enables man to enjoy many

different types of sport and physical activities. God always intended that man should live in comfort and that he should enjoy physical aspects of life.

IV TO ENJOY MENTAL LIFE

The great intellectual capacity of man enables him to enjoy many different types of mental activity such as reading, writing, learning, talking and thinking.

V TO ENJOY SPIRITUAL LIFE

The most important aspect of man's design is the potential to have a knowledge of God and to have a relationship with God. It is ironic how many people put great effort into achieving physical fitness at the gym and mental fitness at university and yet they will totally neglect their spiritual state throughout their lives. It is also very sad that the modern education system teaches children that they are just animals, because this teaching discourages children from seeking to know God. It is interesting to note that modern man believes that humans are just 'a little above the beasts'. In contrast, Psalm 8 teaches that man is made 'a little lower than the angels' (Psalm 8:5).

Notes on Chapter 10

1   **Guiness, A.,** *Marvels and mysteries of the human mind,* p. 117, 1992.

2   **Henry, M.,** *Bible commentary,* Mac Donald Press, Vol. 6, Romans 1:20, p. 370.

3   **Henry, M.,** *op. cit..,* Vol. 3, Psalm 19:1, p. 301, 1710.

The unique beauty of man

Leah's eyes were delicate, but Rachel was beautiful of form and appearance (Genesis 29:17).

The Bible makes more reference to the beauty of the human being than to any other part of creation. The unique and delicate beauty of the human being demonstrates that humans have not evolved from apes. This chapter describes how different parts of the human body have a unique and delicate beauty.

Even though the human body has been affected by the Fall and often contains blemishes due to aging and hereditary defects, it is still possible to see clear evidence of beauty in the human body. It is a difficult task to articulate why something is beautiful because the perception of beauty is partly an emotional and personal response. This chapter discusses 20 beautiful features of the human body and gives objectives reasons for the beauty.

11.1 The face

The face is arguably the most important and beautiful part of the body because it is the main source of identity for a person and because it contains several intricate features. When a person smiles, whether they are a child or adult, this is a particularly beautiful sight. The beauty of the face is referred to in several places in the book of the Song of Solomon (Song of Solomon 1:15, 4:1–3, 5:12–13 and 7:4).

I UNIQUE EYES

One of the things which makes eyes beautiful is the colouring in the iris. The most common colours of the eyes are brown and blue although some eyes are blue-green or brown-green. Blue and green colours are remarkable because such colours do not appear anywhere else on the body. Blue and green are produced when there is a lack of pigment in the iris and light is scattered. Not only do the eyes have distinctive colouring but they also sometimes have a shiny or sparkly appearance. A unique feature of human eyes is that the whites of the eyes are clearly visible, as shown in Fig. 11–1. With animals such as apes, the eye openings are too small to show the whites of the eyes, as shown in Fig. 11–2. The whites of human eyes are beautiful because they emphasise the colouring of the iris. The whites of the eyes also enable eye contact to be made with a person from a distance. When you look at someone across a room, you can tell if they are

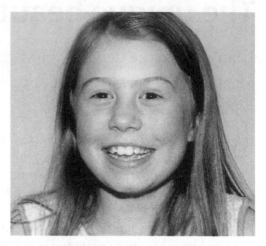

Fig. 11–1 The human head

looking at you because the whites of the eyes make it clear where the eyes are looking. Such eye contact would be much more difficult or impossible if it were not for the whites of the eyes.

II NEAT EYEBROWS

Eyebrows have a function of keeping perspiration out of the eyes. However, eyebrows are very appropriately and beautifully shaped because they are narrow and located neatly on the ridge of the eye socket. According to evolution, the eyebrows appeared by genetic mistakes. However, if this were so, then one would not expect eyebrows to be so neatly designed.

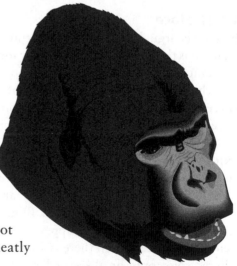

Fig. 11–2 An ape's head

III DISTINCTIVE NOSE

One of the beautiful features of the human nose is that it is very distinctive. In the case of apes, the nose is very flat on the face and it is not always clear where the nose starts and finishes. In contrast, the human nose has a very distinctive outline. Even though the nose is distinctive, it blends in with the face perfectly. The top of the nose gradually tapers into the forehead and the sides of the nose curve gently into the cheeks. The nose also blends in with the eyes and eyebrows. In Fig. 11–1 it can be observed how the curves formed by the two eyebrows (and top edge of the eye sockets) flow into the two curves formed by the two sides of the nose. This alignment cannot be explained by chance!

IV SOFT AND ROUNDED LIPS

The lips are a very important feature in the human face because their colour and thickness make the mouth distinctive. Without the lips, the mouth would be just a narrow slit in the face and would not be easy to recognise. However, the lips make the mouth as distinctive as the other features of the face, as shown in Fig. 11–1. The lips are beautiful because they are very rounded, curved and soft. The upper lip is particularly beautiful because it contains a central dip underneath the nose.

V LEVEL TEETH

Humans have a very neat and level row of teeth compared to the teeth of animals. Even though humans have canine teeth, these are approximately the same height as the other teeth in the mouth. Almost every carnivorous or omnivorous animal has canine teeth which are longer than the other teeth. The human mouth can also close so that the lower teeth are exactly under the upper teeth. The even arrangement of teeth and alignment of upper and lower jaws means that humans have a beautiful smile, as shown in Fig. 11–1.

VI ROUNDED CHEEKS AND CHIN

The cheeks and chin are beautiful because they are rounded and smooth. Some people even have a dimple in their cheeks and/or chin.

VII INTRICATE EARS

The human ear has many intricate curves and foldings. Another desirable feature of the human ear is that it is parallel and close to the head rather than sticking out as with many animals. The closeness of the ear is important because it does not spoil the oval outline of the head.

VIII WELL SPACED FACIAL FEATURES

The features of the face are spaced evenly with the mouth being a similar distance away from the nose as the eyes are from the nose. The ears, eyes, nose and mouth are also well proportioned because each has a similar size and because they are the right size for the face. In contrast, apes often have facial features which are not so well spaced and sized.

11.2 The neck and head

The beauty of the human neck, head and hair is referred to in several places in the book of the Song of Solomon (Song of Solomon 4:1, 4:4, 5:11, 7:5).

I BLENDED NECK

The human neck is beautiful because it is slender and because it blends in gently with the torso and head. The neck also performs the important function of separating the head from the torso so that the head is a completely distinct feature, as shown in Fig. 11–1. In the case of apes, the head merges in with the body and the head is not so distinct, as shown in Fig. 11–2. It is actually an advantage for apes not to have a slender neck because a slender neck can be a point of physical weakness. The delicate neck of the human being is not what would be expected if humans had evolved to be tough hunters.

II ROUNDED HEAD

The human head has a very rounded shape when viewed from any angle. In contrast, apes have a head which is an irregular shape, as shown in Fig. 11–2.

III FINE HAIR

One of the beautiful aspects of human hair is that it is very fine. Another aspect of the beauty of hair is that it comes in a great variety of colours and forms. Hair occurs naturally in a range of colours from blond to ginger to black. It also comes in a range of forms from straight to tight curls. The fast rate of growth of hair on the human head is remarkable because the rest of the body does not have hair which grows continually. The Apostle Paul teaches that the hair is the glory of the woman (1 Corinthians 11:15). The Bible also says that the splendour of old people is their grey hair (Proverbs 20:29).

IV ACCURATE HAIRLINE
Not only can the hair on the head grow very long but it also has a perfect hairline. The hairline is the right distance above the eyes and it neatly goes around the ears and round the back of the head. It is difficult to think of any improvements that could be made to the location of hair on the head. Even if one could think of a reason why hair would just appear on the head by accident, one would not expect that accident to produce a perfect hairline.

11.3 The body
The beauty of the human body is referred to in the Song of Solomon 5:14–15 and 7:1–2.

I UPRIGHT STATURE
The upright stature of the human body is very elegant because it produces a very straight body. In contrast, apes have a permanently bent back with bent legs.

II WELL PROPORTIONED BODY
The human body has beautiful proportions. The legs are approximately half the total height of the body and when the arms are outstretched, the distance from fingertip to fingertip is approximately the same as the total height of the person. In contrast, apes have legs which are much less than half of their height. In addition, when apes stretch out their arms, the distance from fingertip to fingertip is much greater than the total height of the ape. At the end of the chapter it will be shown that the body contains some special geometrical properties.

III SMOOTH CURVES

One of the most beautiful aspects of the human body is that it is very curvaceous and rounded. Whilst both the body of the man and the woman are beautiful, there are reasons why the body of the woman is particularly beautiful. One reason is that the woman has a smoother body profile due to finer skin, smaller muscles and lack of body hair. There are several references to beautiful women in the book of Genesis including Sarai (Genesis 12:11), Rebekah (Genesis 26:7) and Rachel (Genesis 29:17). In Genesis 29:17, Rachel is said to be beautiful of form and appearance. The beauty of the female body is mentioned graphically in the Song of Solomon where we read, 'The curves of your thighs are like jewels, the work of the hands of a skilful workman. Your navel is a rounded goblet; it lacks no blended beverage. Your waist is a heap of wheat set about with lilies.' (Song of Solomon 7:1–2). It is interesting that the terms 'curves', 'rounded' and 'blended' are used in the Song of Solomon because these are some of the most important terms used in modern aesthetics design. The use of such aesthetic terms is not surprising because the body represents a model of great beauty.

IV WAISTLINE

One of the most beautiful features of the woman is the waistline which is unique in creation. The Song of Solomon only mentions the waist in connection with the beauty of the woman. It is interesting to note that modern designers often try to create a waistline in products such as bottles (e.g. coke) and cars (e.g. Peugeot) in order to mimic the beauty of the woman's body.

V FINE SKIN

Another beautiful aspect of skin is its exceptional smoothness and softness. The human being is unique in being naked and having fine skin. The nakedness of the human allows the exact profile of the body to be seen in detail. An important feature of skin is that it is very elastic and able to stretch over the body when the body is moving and bending. In contrast, when engineers surround a joint with covers, the covers have to fold and crinkle when the joint moves.

11.4 Human voice

The human voice arguably produces the most beautiful sounds in creation. In contrast, apes can only produce crude grunts and roars. Evolution has no explanation for the beauty of the human voice.

I PURE SOUND

The human vocal cords and vocal tract are finely tuned to produce beautiful sounds. The quality of sound produced by a professional singer can rival the sounds made by the best man-made instruments. This is one reason why many great composers have used the human voice in some of their finest works. For example, Handel's *Messiah*, Mendelssohn's *Hear my prayer* and Stainer's *Crucifixion* are some of the most beautiful pieces of music ever produced.

II WIDE RANGE OF PITCH

A good voice has a range of pitch of about three octaves although some trained singers can go well beyond this. When considering a range of different singers, which includes bass and soprano (or treble), the possible range of pitch is at least four octaves. It is interesting to note that a typical wind instrument like a flute has a range of pitch of about three octaves. By having a potential range of at least four octaves (about two octaves above and below middle C), human singing can involve quite complex and sophisticated melodies and harmonies.

III FINE CONTROL

As well as producing pure sounds, trained singers can also vary their sounds precisely to produce fast-moving music and subtle changes of expression.

11.5 Mathematical beauty

Since the time of the ancient Greek philosophers, mathematicians have noticed that the human body appears to contain important mathematical properties. These mathematical properties have no evolutionary explanation.

I GOLDEN RATIO

Some scientists believe that the human body is modelled on the Golden

Ratio. The Golden Ratio is produced when two related and principal dimensions have a ratio of 1.618 to 1. This ratio is special because it is the only ratio where the ratio of the larger dimension to the smaller dimension (i.e. 1.618 to 1) is the same as the ratio of the sum of the two dimensions to the larger dimension (i.e. 2.618 to 1.618). Even though most people do not know about the existence of the Golden Ratio, studies have shown that most people find objects more beautiful when they contain the Golden Ratio. The reason for this is that the human eye can subconsciously recognise the equality of ratios in the principal dimensions of an object. The Golden Ratio has been used much in Greek sculpture and architecture and it is still used in modern architecture and design. There are even plastic surgeons who try to achieve the Golden Ratio when adjusting the features of the face in plastic surgery.

Even though there is much variation in the shape and size of people, many of the principal features of the human being do appear to be based on the Golden Ratio. The human face is believed to contain many Golden Ratios in the size and layout of the different features. The human face itself fits inside a Golden Rectangle because the ratio of the height to the width of the face is approximately equal to the Golden Ratio. The face shown in Fig. 11–1 fits inside a rectangle which is very close to a Golden Rectangle.

II CIRCLE AND SQUARE

The human body can fit very elegantly inside a circle and a square. This was famously demonstrated in the drawing of the Vitruvian man by Leonardo da Vinci. In this drawing, a naked man is drawn with his legs and arms in two positions. In one position, the body has the posture of a 'star jump' and the body fits exactly inside a circle with the navel exactly at the centre of the circle and the feet and hands at the edge of the circle. In the other position, the legs are straight and the arms are outstretched horizontally and the man fits exactly inside a square. Leonardo da Vinci also used Golden Ratios in his drawing of the man. One example of the Golden Ratio is the position of the navel. The total height of the man divided by the distance from the navel to the bottom of the feet is exactly equal to the Golden Ratio.

11.6 Comparison of humans with apes

Table 11–1 summarises the 20 differences between humans and apes discussed in this chapter. Of course, apes have a type of beauty of their own which is in keeping with their wild existence. However, the human being has an unmatched delicate beauty. The gulf between the beauty of humans and apes shows that humans have not gradually evolved from apes.

Table 11–1 Comparison of external features in humans and apes

FEATURE	HUMANS	APES
Neck	Delicate	No neck
Head	Rounded	Irregular shape
Hair	Fine hair	Coarse fur
Hairline	Accurate	No hairline
Eyes	Whites visible	Whites not visible
Eyebrows	Neat	None
Nose	Distinct	Not distinct
Lips	Soft and distinct	No lips
Teeth	Even	Uneven
Cheeks	Rounded	Crude
Ears	Delicate folds	Coarse folds
Facial features	Even spacing	Uneven spacing
Body	Upright	Bent
Body	Well proportioned	Poor proportions
Body	Curvaceous	Barrel-shaped
Body	Waist on woman	No waist
Skin	Fine	Coarse fur
Voice	Pure sound	Crude grunts
Voice	Fine control	Poor control
Voice	Wide pitch range	Limited pitch range

11.7 The beauty of the human being

It is very interesting to note that when film-makers create alien beings which are slightly different to human beings, the result is always to produce something less beautiful. The reason for this is that the human being is a perfect model of beauty. There is nothing that man can suggest to improve the beauty of the human body.

The human being is arguably the most beautiful creature that God has made. In Chapter 6 it was noted that, in general, birds rarely have a beautiful voice *and* a beautiful appearance. In contrast, humans have both a beautiful voice and a beautiful appearance.

The features of the human body are so beautiful and co-ordinated that they cannot be explained by mechanical function. Indeed, the human body has many delicate features that are a hindrance to survival in the wild. The theory of evolution has no explanation for the delicate beauty of man. The smiling face of a young child alone is enough to demonstrate the absurdity of the theory of evolution.

The biblical creation account

For in six days the Lord made the heavens and the earth, the sea, and all that is in them, and rested the seventh day (Exodus 20:11).

Genesis 1 gives a historical record of the creation of the entire universe, describing in detail the order and length of creation. This chapter shows why the order and length of the creation week are very logical and encouraging because they demonstrate that the earth and mankind are at the centre of God's purposes in the universe.

12.1 Six-day creation

The first chapter of Genesis describes the following order of creation:

Day One: Time, space (heavens), earth, water and light
Day Two: Atmosphere (heaven) and clouds
Day Three: Land and plants
Day Four: Sun, moon and stars
Day Five: Sea creatures and birds
Day Six: Land creatures and Adam and Eve
Day Seven: Day of rest

There is much support within the Bible itself for the Genesis account being a literal account of creation in six 24-hour days. The book of Exodus states that the seven-day week is based on God's work of creation in one week (Exodus 20:11). In the book of Acts we read that there have been prophets since the world began (Acts 3:21) and the Lord Jesus Himself said that since the creation of the world there have been male and female (Mark 10:6). These statements that mankind has existed from the very beginning of creation imply that the creation of the earth took days and not millions of years. It is also important to note that the apostle Paul taught that there was significance in the order of creation of the man and the woman (1 Timothy

2:13). Since Paul believed in the order of creation of the man and the woman, which is a relatively small part of the creation account, there is no doubt that he believed in the order of the creation days.

One of the most important things to remember when considering the biblical creation account is that God is infinite in power. Whereas man is limited in what he can make and how he can make it, God is not limited at all. Since God was able to create the universe in any way He wanted, and since the Bible declares that He created it in a certain way, it must be concluded that Genesis 1 is a true and accurate record of how the universe was made.

12.2 A universe for mankind

There are two commonly asked questions about the creation week. The first question is: Why did not God make the sun and stars on the first day before making the earth? The answer to this question is that the sun and stars could not have been made on Day One because there was nothing for them to shine on. The earth is centre-stage of the universe and mankind is at the very centre of God's purposes in the universe. Therefore, it is entirely logical that the method of creation should reflect that the earth is a unique life-bearing planet and that the only purpose of the sun and stars is to serve the earth and mankind. The second question is this: Why should it take three days to make the earth and then only one day to make the stars of the entire universe? The reason why the earth took three times longer to make than the stars is that the earth is of far more importance than the stars. The earth is the unique home of life in the universe and the home deserves more attention than the spotlights on that home. The uniqueness of the earth is confirmed in Isaiah 45:18 where we read that the earth was specially formed to be inhabited. When it is appreciated that all things were designed and created for the sake of mankind then it becomes clear that the order of creation is not strange at all but actually a great encouragement.

The great theologian John Calvin said this about the order of creation:

God Himself has shown by the order of creation that He created all things for man's sake. For it is not without significance that He divided the making of the universe into six days [Gen 1:31], even though it would have been no more difficult for Him to have completed in one moment ...But He willed to commend His providence and fatherly solicitude toward us in that, before He fashioned man, He prepared everything He foresaw would be useful and salutary for him.[1]

Calvin makes the crucial point that God 'created all things for man's sake'. One of the key differences between atheism and Christianity is that atheism considers man as utterly insignificant whilst the Bible considers man at the centre of God's purposes. Therefore, the man-centred biblical creation account is completely inconsistent with modern atheistic philosophy. However, the biblical creation account is entirely consistent with biblical teaching on God's purposes in the universe. The following sections look briefly at each of the creation days to see how the creation account is man-centred.

12.3 Day One

The first verse of the Bible teaches that the only physical matter created on the first day was a water-covered earth (Genesis 1:1–2). The space of the universe (the heavens) was also created on the first day. It is important to note that whilst the entire space of the universe was created on the first day of creation, this space contained only the water-covered earth because the sun, moon and stars were created on the fourth day[2] (Genesis 1:14). God also made light on Day One of creation.

That God chose to spend the first day of creation making *only* the foundations of the earth shows that His purpose from the very beginning was to make a home for mankind. To illustrate this point, consider what happens when a house is built. It is normal practice to start with the foundations of the house rather than with the gardens and outbuildings even though the house may occupy a relatively small area of the total space available. The reason for this is that the house is of much more value and importance than the garden. In a similar way, God worked on the foundations of the earth because the earth is the home of mankind and therefore the most significant part of the universe.

The Bible describes God as being a deliberate and careful Creator. In the book of Job we read that God determined the measurements of the foundations of the earth and that He stretched a line upon it (Job 38:5). In the book of Proverbs we read that '…when He drew a circle on the face of the deep…When He marked out the foundations of the earth, then I was beside Him as a master craftsman' (Proverbs 8:27–30). The description of God as a great craftsman[3] measuring out the dimensions of the foundations of the earth shows the folly of theistic evolution because a craftsman works in a way which is the opposite of the process of evolution. The account of the first day of creation shows that God did not create using random natural processes but that He created in a careful and supernatural way.

12.4 Day Two

On the second day of creation God made the sky which includes the earth's atmosphere and clouds (Genesis 1:6–8). It is interesting to note that until modern times there was no obvious reason to believe that there was a sky at all. This is because at night-time it looks as if there is no difference between the space near to the earth and that which is far away. Only in modern times have observations shown that there is a very real atmosphere that clings to the earth. The fact that the book of Genesis highlights the sky as being a major part of creation, and that it was written thousands of years ago, is evidence that the Bible is not the work of mankind but has been inspired by God.

The second day of creation involved the next phase of mankind's home being completed. That God chose to spend a whole day making the earth's atmosphere, with its air and clouds, shows that these things are very important to mankind. As before, this can be illustrated with the analogy of a family home. When the foundations and shell of a man-made house have been built, there are still many important tasks for the builder to undertake such as installing the heating system and the water supply. Such systems help to make life in the home more pleasant and convenient. In a similar way, the earth's atmosphere gives a pleasant environment which has the right temperature and a convenient supply of fresh water. The Bible speaks in detail of how the weather system has been deliberately designed for life on earth (Job 36:27–28 and Psalm 104:10–13). The account of the second day of creation shows again that God created the earth in a careful and supernatural way.

12.5 Day Three

On the third day of creation God made the earth suitable for the habitation of mankind by making dry land (Genesis 1:9) and by making plants

(Genesis 1:11). It should be noted that the plants were mature plants because Adam was able to live on the fruit of the land immediately. This feature again reveals God as a craftsman who does not need to wait long periods to achieve His goals. The order of creation again shows that God has made the earth as a home for mankind. As before, this can be illustrated by analogy with a family home. When the structure and services of a house have been completed, it is usual to spend much time fitting the rooms with carpets and furniture and decorating the walls. In a similar way, God spent the third day of creation making the earth habitable by creating dry land. Having made the rooms of the earth, God then created plants to stock the earth with food and provide beauty. Matthew Henry said this about the creation of the earth:

The world is a great house, consisting of upper and lower stories, the structure stately and magnificent, uniform and convenient, and every room well and wisely furnished.[4]

At the end of the third day the earth was indeed a magnificent house, with the upstairs (the sky) being a wonderful home for birds and the downstairs (the land) being a wonderful home for mankind.

12.6 Day Four

Having prepared a wonderful home for mankind in the first three days, God then made lights to shine upon the earth on Day Four of creation (Genesis 1:15). Given that the sun, moon and stars exist only to be of service to the earth, it makes sense that they should be created *after* the earth. To illustrate this point, consider what happens when a jewel is prepared for display. When the jewel is being manufactured it is usual to put it under the light of the craftsman's special work-light. Only when the jewel is finished is it specially mounted and given display lights for viewing. In a similar way, God made the earth in His own supernatural light in three days, and then put natural lights in place on the fourth day to display the earth. This is what Thomas Watson says about the fourth day in his *body of divinity*:

The heavens were bespangled with the sun, moon, and stars, that so the world's beauty might be beheld and admired.[5]

It is amazing to think that the purpose of the trillions of stars in the universe is to light up the earth and to serve the needs of mankind! The fourth day must have been an amazing day when the lights of the universe suddenly lit up the beautiful earth. Matthew Henry said the following about the stars:

The lights of heaven…shine for us, for our pleasure and advantage… The lights of heaven are made to serve us, and they do it faithfully, and shine in their season, without fail…[6]

It is important to point out that the earth would have received light the same day that the stars were made, even though light now takes a very long time to travel from distant stars to the earth. The reason why the stars were able to shine light on the earth so quickly is that God made a *mature* universe. The concept of mature creation is seen throughout the creation week. The creation week involved the supernatural creation of a mature earth, mature plants and mature creatures. Therefore, everything in creation would have had an apparent age, even though it was actually brand new. Since God was the very Creator of the stars it would have been a trivial matter for Him to make starlight reach the earth on the fourth day of creation. Indeed, God not only created stars and light but also the physical laws that govern the way stars and light work. A more detailed discussion about the creation of stars on the fourth day of creation is given in the reference.[7]

That God should fill every corner of a vast universe with trillions of lights just for the earth seems very strange to modern man because it is infinitely beyond what is functionally required. According to the logic of modern man, if the stars were really created so as to give light on the earth, then there should be only a few thousand of them because that would be enough to make a starry night-time sky. However, God chose to demonstrate His infinite goodness and power by making trillions of stars just to shine on the earth. It is very sad that modern man points to the trillions of stars as evidence for atheism and the big bang theory when such stars actually demonstrate God's wonderful fatherly love towards mankind!

12.7 Day Five
Having finished the beautiful earth and made lights to shine upon it, God

then created sea creatures and birds on the fifth day (Genesis 1:20–23). Once again the order of creation contradicts the theory of evolution because all of the plants were completed before any creatures appeared and because the birds were made before any of the land animals. However, once again we see a perfect order because creatures were put into a completed home and because the creatures that are most like man came on the sixth day when mankind was made.

It is interesting to note that God commanded that there should be an *abundance* of living creatures in the waters (Genesis 1:20). Here we see God's intention that there should be extreme diversity in the earth from the beginning. Also notice that God also gave a command for the fish and birds to *fill* the earth (Genesis 1:22). Here we see that God always intended to have creatures in every corner of the earth. Modern discoveries about the existence of many creatures in the extreme environments of the earth have demonstrated the spectacular truth of these verses.

12.8 Day Six

On the sixth day of creation God made the land creatures and Adam and Eve. It is significant that man was the very last part of creation to be made so that he was introduced into a home that was complete in every way. It is also important to note that the whole creation had an appearance of age with fully mature plants and creatures even though the universe was only six days old.

It is very significant that the Bible goes into detail about how and when man was made. God created the universe by speaking commands, whereas He *formed* man from the dust of the ground (Genesis 2:7). It is also significant that God breathed into man the breath of life. Such an intimate method of creation demonstrates that man is a special creature made in the image of God (Genesis 1:27). There is also significance in the order of creation of the man and woman. God made the man first to show that he had the responsibility for leading the family. God made the woman from one of the ribs of Adam to show that the woman was not inferior to man but intimately related to him. After the creation of the man and woman, God blessed man and instructed him to fill the earth and to have dominion over it. Such a blessing and instruction confirms once again that the earth was made for mankind.

12.9 Day Seven

Having made the universe and living beings in six days, God then chose to have a day of rest on the seventh day. Since God is infinite in power, it was not necessary for Him to rest on the seventh day. However, God had a loving reason for resting on the seventh day because He knew it would be a great benefit for man to have a day of rest. Having a day of rest not only helps people to rest from work but also helps them to have particularly concentrated thoughts of God on one day in every seven. It is significant that a seven-day week is observed throughout the world. The only explanation for such a worldwide custom is that God did indeed make the world in six days followed by a day of rest. Even though the seventh day of the week used to be the day of rest, this situation has changed since the resurrection of the Lord Jesus Christ. Since Christ rose on the first day of the week, the Lord's Day is now on the *first* day of the week, which is Sunday.

12.10 Made wonderfully

Genesis 1 shows that the world is not just wonderfully made but that it was made in a wonderful way. The method of creation is an encouragement because the length of the creation process and the order of creation demonstrate that the universe was made for the sake of mankind. The method of creation is also an encouragement because it demonstrates God's infinite power.

THE LENGTH OF CREATION

The fact that the creation week lasted seven days helps us to understand and appreciate the creation process because it can be related to our own seven-day week. The biblical creation account also encourages us to keep a day of rest. John Calvin says this about the number of days of creation:

Whence it also appears, that God always had respect to the welfare of men. I have said above, that six days were employed in the formation of the world; not that God, to whom one moment is as a thousand years, had need of this succession of time, but that he might engage us in the consideration of his work. He had the same end in view in the appointment of his own rest, for he set apart a day selected out of the remainder for this special use.[8]

It is sad that there are people who do not believe that the creation week was a literal week because, as Calvin points out, the length of creation shows that 'God always had respect to the welfare of men'. Indeed, God deliberately designed the process of creation in order to *be* understandable by mankind!

THE ORDER OF CREATION

The order of creation also reveals God's kindness towards mankind. John Calvin says the following about the order of creation:

But we ought in the very order of things diligently to contemplate God's fatherly love towards mankind, in that he did not create Adam until he had lavished upon the universe all manner of good things. For if he had put him in an earth as yet sterile and empty, if he had given him life before light, he would have seemed to provide insufficiently for his welfare. Now when he disposed the movements of the sun and stars to human uses, filled the earth, waters, and air with living things, and brought forth an abundance of fruits to suffice as foods, in this assuming the responsibility of a foreseeing and diligent father of the family he shows his wonderful goodness towards us.[9]

It is ironic that some people find the order of creation strange when the order of creation actually reveals God's infinite goodness towards mankind!

THE METHOD OF CREATION

The Bible teaches that the method of creation described in Genesis 1 should lead to great respect for God: 'Let all the earth fear the Lord; Let all the inhabitants of the world stand in awe of Him. For He spoke, and it was done; He commanded, and it stood fast' (Psalm 33:8–9). When we consider *how* God created the entire universe out of nothing simply by verbal commands, it becomes clear that He is infinite in power and wisdom and this demands that we stand in awe of Him.

One of the reasons why modern man does not want to believe in creation is that this belief automatically leads to an acknowledgement that God is Lord over all. The influence of evolution is also seen in many professing Christian people in the form of theistic evolution. The effect of theistic evolution is to deny that God has been supernaturally or closely involved in creation and this prevents people from standing so much in awe of Him or seeing Him as a loving Father. Only those who believe fully in the biblical accounts of creation can really appreciate God's power.

12.11 God's fatherly love in Genesis 1

The theory of evolution has led to widespread disrespect for the account of creation in Genesis 1. This is very sad because Genesis 1 reveals that God has infinite wisdom and infinite fatherly love towards mankind. In the book of Job we are told how, at the creation of the foundations of the earth, the morning stars sang together and the sons of God (i.e. angels) shouted for joy (Job 38:7). When we read Genesis 1, we should be thrilled to read about the details of the origins of the universe and how God worked so skilfully in creating a wonderful world for mankind.

Notes on Chapter 12

1   **Calvin, J.,** *Institutes of the Christian religion 1*, Westminster, Chapter 14, pp. 181–182, 1960.

2   The Bible refers to three heavens; the first heaven is the sky (Genesis 1:8), the second heaven is the space of the universe (Genesis 1:1) and the third heaven is the spiritual heaven where God dwells (2 Corinthians 12:20). Even though the second heaven can sometimes include the stars of the universe, in Genesis 1:1 it only refers to the empty space of the universe since the stars were specifically made on the fourth day (Genesis 1:15). The fact that the first heaven refers to the 'space' of the earth's atmosphere shows that the word 'heaven' can refer to space alone. A more detailed discussion of Genesis 1:1 can be found in the Genesis commentary by Morris. (Morris, H., *Genesis commentary*, Baker books, Genesis 1:1, pp. 161–162, 1960.)

3   The New King James Version uses the term Master Craftsman but the Authorised Version does not.

4   **Henry, M.,** *Bible commentary*, Mac Donald, Genesis 1:1, p. 2.

5   **Watson, T.,** *A body of divinity* (1692), The Banner of Truth Trust, Chapter 13 'The Creation', p. 114, 1965.

6   **Henry, M.,** *op. cit.*, Genesis 1:15, p. 7.

7   **Burgess, S.C.,** *He made the stars also*, Day One, Epsom, Surrey, 2001.

8   **Calvin, J.,** *Genesis*, Banner of Truth, Genesis 1:28, p. 105, 1965.

9   **Calvin, J.,** *Institutes of the Christian religion* Vol 1, Westminster, Chapter 14, pp. 161–162.

Answering objections to the design argument

For every house is built by someone, but He who built all things is God (Hebrews 3:4).

T he Design Argument argues that design reveals a Designer. Following modern discoveries about the staggering complexity of life, the Design Argument is stronger than ever before. The only way that the evolutionist can now argue against the Design Argument is to object to the whole concept of design. This chapter starts by giving a brief historical background to the Design Argument. It then gives answers to seven of the most common objections to the Design Argument.

13.1 Historical background to the Design Argument

The Design Argument (sometimes called the *teleological* argument) is not a man-made argument but a biblical argument. The Design Argument can be found in the Old Testament and New Testament. The psalmist says: 'The heavens declare the glory of God; and the firmament shows His handiwork.' (Psalm 19:1). The apostle Paul says: 'For since the creation of the world His [God's] invisible attributes are clearly seen, being understood by the things that are made, even His eternal power and Godhead, so that they are without excuse.' (Romans 1:20).

Theologians sometimes illustrate the importance of the Design Argument by pointing out that there are two books which reveal God. The Bible is the book of 'theology' and nature is the book of 'natural theology'. Theologians also sometimes refer to the two universes. Nature is the 'physical universe' and the Bible is the 'spiritual universe'.

The Design Argument has been used down through the ages to argue for a Designer. In 1692, over 300 years ago, the puritan writer Thomas Watson presented the Design Argument eloquently as follows:

If one should go into a far country, and see stately edifices, he would never imagine that they could build themselves, but that there had been some artificer to raise such goodly structures; so this great fabric of the world could not create itself, it must have some builder or maker, and that is God.[1]

It is interesting to note that these words were written over 150 years before the publication of *Origin of Species* by Charles Darwin. This shows that there has always been a need to convince people that there is a Creator to whom we must give an account. The quotation also shows that the main purpose of the Design Argument is to present positive evidence for a Creator regardless of whether there is any man-made theory of origins. One of the most famous presenters of the Design Argument was William Paley. In 1802 Paley wrote a book called *Natural Theology* in which he gave the famous analogy of finding a watch to illustrate the Design Argument:

In crossing a heath…suppose I had found a watch upon the ground, and it should be inquired how the watch happened to be in that place ….the inference we think is inevitable, that the watch must have had a maker—that there must have existed, at some time and at some place or other, an artificer or artificers who formed it for the purpose which we find it actually answer, who completely comprehended its construction and designed its use.[2]

Paley showed that creatures and plants contain evidence of design that is even more compelling than that of a well-engineered watch. Considering that knowledge of biological systems was relatively simple in Paley's day, his arguments for a designer are very good. Just over 100 years ago the great scientist Lord Kelvin said this about the evidence of design in nature:

Overwhelmingly strong proofs of intelligent design lie around us … the atheistic idea is so non-sensical that I cannot put it into words.[3]

Lord Kelvin, like other great scientists of his time, was fully aware of the theory of evolution but was greatly opposed to it. Today there are still many scientists who believe that the world has a Designer.[4] Professor

McIntosh has recently said that the Design Argument is the most unassailable argument against evolution.[5]

13.2 Objection: Only evolution is 'naturalistic'

Many modern scientists assume that evolution is credible and that creation is non-credible because evolution involves a naturalistic explanation of origins whereas creation ultimately involves a supernatural explanation. This is why Sir Julian Huxley said 'modern science must rule out special creation or divine guidance'. Sadly, many scientists have followed this irrational advice and have rejected special creation without even beginning to consider the evidence for design. This is also why virtually all biology books in schools and universities teach evolution without stating even the possibility of design. If scientists did not rule out special creation, there is every reason to believe that many modern scientists would acknowledge the overwhelming evidence for design. For example, if scientists did not rule out special creation then they would not automatically associate similarities in creatures with evidence for evolution because they would realise that similarity could be evidence for design.

To rule out the possibility of a Designer is ironic because this represents a sweeping decision that breaks all the rules of good science. Sound science involves making decisions on the basis of solid evidence. However, evolutionists rule out a Designer without considering any evidence at all! Evolutionists argue that their justification for ruling out special creation is that special creation involves supernatural and not natural processes. However, no one has ever shown that supernatural processes do not belong in the universe. In fact, it can be argued that there are several miracles that are very apparent in nature. The very existence of matter/energy is a miracle because matter/energy cannot be created or destroyed by any natural process. The existence of time is a miracle because time has no beginning. The existence of the universe is a miracle because space has no end. Therefore, it is actually a great mistake to conclude that there cannot be any such thing as a miracle in nature. Also, belief in supernatural creation is perfectly compatible with scientific principles.

Not only do evolutionists make the mistake of assuming that special creation is unscientific, but they also make the mistake of assuming that evolution does not require faith. To assume that there must be a naturalistic explanation to origins amounts to making a *big* step of faith. Evolution involves faith that everything can be traced back to a natural first cause. In fact, since no one has seen evolution happen, the evolutionist must have 'blind faith'. The fact that evolution involves faith is shown clearly in a highly respected school textbook on advanced-level biology:

…some people could not even accept that the first organisms to evolve on this planet arose by spontaneous generation, preferring to believe that life was brought here by meteorites from other planets. For various reasons this is most unlikely, and we are therefore forced to conclude that life originally arose by spontaneous generation, even though the process appears not to be repeatable today.[6]

Notice in this quotation that the author admits that the spontaneous generation of life appears 'not to be repeatable today'. This situation is very embarrassing for the evolutionist because modern scientists now have very sophisticated equipment that is well capable of simulating processes that do occur in nature. Also notice in this quotation how the author says that we are 'forced' to conclude that life arose spontaneously because it is unlikely that life came from outer space. The key point is that people are only 'forced' to conclude that life arose spontaneously if they have rejected the idea of a Creator God and have faith that there must be a naturalistic explanation to origins!

13.3 Objection: God could have used evolution to create the universe

There are many people who object to the Design Argument because they believe that God could have used evolution to create life and the universe. Such a belief is called *theistic evolution*. There are several reasons why God did not use evolution to create the universe, including:

(i)   The Bible teaches that God created the first man from the dust of the ground in one step (Genesis 2:7) whereas evolution teaches that mankind came from monkeys.

(ii)   The Bible teaches that the original creation was perfect at the end of the creation week with no death of creatures (Genesis 1:31) whereas evolution involves the death of creatures and a violent struggle for existence before the Fall.

(iii) The Bible teaches that God worked like a craftsman (Proverbs 8:30) whereas the theory of evolution is based on chance mistakes.

(iv) The Bible teaches that God is infinite in wisdom (Psalm 147:5) whereas evolution involves the most clumsy process possible for producing life.

To believe that God used evolution involves disbelieving the Bible and putting faith in the beliefs of atheistic scientists. Indeed, the teaching of evolution in schools and universities is not based on real evidence but is a reflection of the atheistic beliefs of western society.

13.4 Objection: What is the origin of the Designer?

Another objection to the Design Argument is that if there is a Designer, then there is still the unanswered question of the origin of the Designer. Richard Dawkins puts this objection in the following way:

To explain the origin of the DNA/protein machine by invoking a supernatural Designer is to explain precisely nothing, for it leaves unexplained the origin of the Designer. You have to say something like 'God was always here', and if you allow yourself that kind of lazy way out, you might as well just say 'DNA was always there', or 'life was always there', and be done with it.[7]

The simple answer to this objection is that even if you cannot explain the existence of the Designer, this does not in any way invalidate the conclusion that there is a Designer! This example again shows how the atheist makes the mistake of assuming that everything *must* be explained by natural causes.

This atheistic and false reasoning can be illustrated by analogy with a man-made device. If someone asked you how a man-made machine came into existence, you would answer that it was the result of the work of human designers even if you did not personally know the designers. Just because you have not explained the origin of the designers does not mean that you have answered incorrectly. If someone criticised you for not assuming a million-year evolution of the machine by random accidents this would be ridiculous because the machine had not evolved! In the same way, it is ridiculous for evolutionists to argue that there must be a completely naturalistic explanation to life on earth just because we cannot explain the origin of the Creator.

The fact that we cannot explain the origin of God is actually quite instructive because God by His very nature does not have an origin. Isaiah tells us that God's name is from everlasting (Isaiah 63:16) and that He inhabits eternity (Isaiah 57:15). Creation shows not just that there is a Designer but that this Designer is eternal.

13.5 Objection: No one has seen God create life

Some people object to the Design Argument because they have never seen life being supernaturally created and have never known anyone capable of supernatural creation. The answer to this objection is that there can still be evidence of design even if we have not seen the act of design. William Paley addresses this objection by using the analogy of the watch:

…Nor would it, I apprehend, weaken the conclusion [i.e. design], that we had never seen a watch made—that we had never known an artist capable of making one.[8]

Just because there is no one around in modern times who has seen God create does not mean that the conclusion of design is any weaker. It is important to note that the first people whom God made would actually have appreciated the fact that they had been supernaturally created. Adam and Eve would have been aware of their lack of human parents (and their lack of a navel!) and therefore would have had physical evidence of God's creative power.

There have also been people who have directly experienced God's supernatural power to create. There were wedding guests who saw the Lord Jesus turn water into wine (John 2:1–11). The Lord Jesus was also seen to bring dead people back to life (John 11:38–44). These are examples of God demonstrating His ability to create instantly.

13.6 Objection: Why does the Designer allow suffering?

A common objection to the Design Argument relates to the amount of suffering and injustice in the world. People reason that if the world had been designed, then the designer would have made the world perfect. The answer to this objection is that the world *was* perfect when God created it. This is why the Bible records that the world was very good at the end of the creation week (Genesis 1:31). Our present world contains suffering only because God cursed the world as a judgement for the rebellion of Adam and Eve. Therefore, the suffering that we see in this world is a result of the sin of mankind and even though we see the effect of the curse on creation, we can still clearly see the hallmarks of an infinitely good, powerful and wise Creator.

It is ironic when suffering is used to criticise Christianity because suffering is essential to the theory of evolution. According to evolution, the suffering that is caused by gene mutation is very necessary because gene mutation drives evolution. In addition, when the strong destroy the weak in nature, this is supposed to be a good thing because it is weeding out the unfit.

Considering the state of the world, the most appropriate question to ask is: Why is God so patient with mankind? People are so rebellious against God and His commands that the world deserves to be ended and judged immediately. The fact that God allows the world to continue, to enable His message of salvation to reach His people, actually demonstrates that God has great mercy and love.

13.7 Objection: Does not the age of the earth support evolution?

Evolutionists claim that the universe is billions of years old and that this provides evidence for evolution and against design. The first point to make here is that even if the universe *was* billions of years old, this would not help the theory of evolution because evolution cannot evolve irreducible systems even in an infinite amount of time. The second point to make is that no one has proved that the earth is very old. Even though dating methods do appear to show that the universe is very old, these methods cannot take account of the supernatural process of creation. To illustrate this point, consider the task of finding out how long a mechanical clock has been ticking. Whilst it is possible to calculate how fast the spring unwinds, it is impossible to calculate how much the clock was wound in the first place since the person who wound up the clock was 'outside' of the clock. In a similar way, since God was 'outside' of the universe when He created it, we cannot determine its age. Even though we can measure how fast the universe is unwinding at the present time, this does not mean that we can extrapolate backwards by billions of years to a so-called Big Bang because we cannot measure when God started the universe.

There are several biblical examples of where God's creation had the *appearance* of age even though it was actually very young. When the stars were created on the fourth day of creation, they were made to shine upon the earth on that day even though light now takes a very long time to reach the earth from distant stars. So, when the universe was only four days old, it would have had the appearance of a vast age if one calculated age by the time it takes for light to reach the earth by natural means. A similar example is found with Adam and Eve. In normal circumstances, a human being takes many years to grow into an adult. However, God miraculously created Adam and Eve as instant adults. So, on the sixth day of creation, Adam and Eve and the rest of creation would already have had the appearance of age.

Other examples of apparent age are found in the New Testament in the miracles of Jesus. It is recorded that the wine that Jesus made was of a very high quality (John 2:1–11). Such wine would have had the appearance of being old even though it was actually brand new. These examples illustrate how supernatural creative events make extrapolation meaningless. The present earth may well have superficial signs of being old but these do not prove age in any way.

13.8 Objection: Do not fossils and dinosaurs support evolution?

If evolution had occurred, then it would be possible to construct an evolutionary tree through the fossil record showing very small changes between different organisms from dead matter to human beings. There would be countless intermediate forms of life between the main classes of animals such as birds, fish, mammals, reptiles and insects. However, the fossil evidence actually shows an abrupt appearance of discrete complex life forms, and scientists such as Professor Gish have shown in great detail how the fossil record actually provides compelling evidence against evolution.[9]

Dinosaurs are sometimes given as an example of evolution at work because it is assumed that they were primitive and that this prevented them from adapting to changing environments. In fact, many scientists now accept that dinosaurs were not primitive at all but very sophisticated and well designed for their environment. It is also accepted that the only sensible explanation for the extinction of the dinosaurs is a major catastrophic event. Therefore, there is no reason why the extinction of the dinosaurs should be an evidence of evolution. The fact that dinosaurs died out is a witness to the decaying of the universe that has taken place since the fall of mankind. Dinosaurs actually give evidence of design.

13.9 The need for faith

The evolutionist often criticises the creationist for having faith in a Creator. However, the evolutionist has at least as much faith in the god of chance. The way in which schools present evolution only in science classes and special creation only in religious education classes is very bad because this gives the misleading impression that evolution is the correct explanation for origins. Either evolution should be taught in religious education classes alongside special creation, or special creation should be taught in science classes alongside the theory of evolution. It may well be that the evolutionist does not want to present evolution alongside special creation because they know that children will instinctively see that evolution is absurd. It is interesting to note that it is generally much harder to convince a child that life has evolved than it is to convince a child that life has been created.

Even though there is overwhelming evidence for design, the Bible teaches that a person must have faith to believe in creation. In the book of Hebrews we read: 'By faith we understand that the worlds were framed by the word of God, so that the things that are seen were not made of the things which are visible.' (Hebrews 11:3). Such a need for faith is due to the fact that the truth about origins cannot be proven. Ultimately, a person must have faith either in creation or faith in man-made theories of origins like evolution. Evolution requires 'great faith in chance' whereas creation requires 'faith in a great God'.

Notes on Chapter 13

1   **Watson, T.,** *A body of divinity* (1692), The Banner of Truth Trust, Chapter 13 'The Creation', p. 114, 1965.

2   **Paley, W.,** *Natural theology: selections,* The Bobbs Merrill company, p. 3, 1963.

3   **Lamont, A.,** *21 Great Scientists who believed*, Creation Science Foundation, p. 37, 1995.

4   **Ashton, J.,** (Editor) *In six days—Why 50 scientists believe in creation*, New Holland, 1999.

5   **McIntosh, A.,** *Genesis for today*, Day One, p. 144, 1998.

6   **Roberts, M.B.V.,** *Biology: a functional approach*, 4th Ed., Nelson, p. 617, 1986.

7   **Dawkins, R.,** *The blind watchmaker*, Penguin, p. 141, 1986.

8   **Paley, W.,** *op. cit.*, p. 12.

9   **Gish, D.,** *Evolution, the challenge of the fossil record*, Master Books, 1985.

Answering the questions of life

For God so loved the world that He gave His only begotten Son, that whoever believes in Him should not perish but have everlasting life (John 3:16).

The origin of life is one of the most important questions of life, but there are other ultimate questions that are related to origins: What is God like? Is the Bible the Word of God? What is the purpose of life? What happens after death? What will happen to the universe? This chapter briefly addresses these ultimate questions.

14.1 What is God like?

The natural world can teach us about some of the attributes of God. The Bible teaches that the natural world particularly reveals God's eternal power and divine nature (Romans 1:20). God's eternal power is seen in the way He has created and sustained the vast universe from the beginning of time. God's divine nature consists of attributes such as goodness, wisdom and fatherly love. Creation reveals these attributes because the world is so intricately and beautifully designed for mankind. The study of God's attributes in nature can be a great encouragement to those who believe in God. For example, being aware of the infinite power of God in creation is an encouragement because it shows that God is able to strengthen a person in any situation. The prophet Isaiah explained this truth vividly when he said: '...The everlasting God, the Lord, the Creator of the ends of the earth, neither faints nor is weary. His understanding is unsearchable. He gives power to the weak, and to those who have no might He increases strength.' (Isaiah 40:28–29). Considering how instructive and encouraging nature can be, it is no wonder that Elihu advised Job to: '...Stand still and consider the wondrous works of God.' (Job 37:14).

The Bible also teaches us what God is like. In fact, the Bible has a much fuller revelation about God than the natural world because the Bible describes God's thoughts and actions from the beginning of the creation of the world. Like nature, the Bible reveals how God has attributes of infinite goodness, power, wisdom and fatherly love. However, the Bible describes many other attributes of God such as holiness, mercy, faithfulness and saving love. God's attributes are also seen in the way that God deals with people. There are many lives that have been transformed by God from a life of rebellion against God to a life that brings glory to God. Such changes show God's mercy, power and grace.

Considering that God is our maker, it should be our desire to find out about Him. People who know God obtain great pleasure from studying God's works. The psalmist expressed this well when he said: 'The works of the Lord are great, studied by all who have pleasure in them' (Psalm 111:2). John Calvin described the study of God as the 'proper business of the whole life'. He wrote:

This is, indeed, the proper business of the whole life, in which men should daily exercise themselves, to consider the infinite goodness, justice, power and wisdom of God, in this magnificent theatre of God.[1]

One of the sad consequences of evolution is that it discourages people from seeking to find out about God. There are many television programmes and books that present in detail the wonder and diversity of life without any reference at all to the God who made all things. Such programmes implicitly teach atheism because they give the impression that there is no God.

It is also very sad that modern man refuses to acknowledge that the world has been made for man. Secular scientists refuse to consider any possibility that bird song has been made for man. It is allowable to consider any physical cause for the beauty of bird song as long as there is no mention of any man-centred purpose. And yet the truth is that the primary purpose of the beauty of bird song is to bring pleasure to man! Even children are now taught that the world has not been designed for mankind. For example, one popular children's encyclopaedia published in the UK says the following:

We love flowers for their colour, shape and scent. Yet their loveliness is not for us; it's to attract small creatures to visit them.[2]

To teach children that the loveliness of flowers is 'not for us' is tantamount to teaching them to be atheists because it is denying the purpose of creation. The truth is that flowers *have* been deliberately made beautiful for us and they teach us that we have a kind and loving heavenly Father! It is outrageous how the education system in the West teaches children that the world has not been made for them to enjoy.

14.2 Is the Bible the Word of God?

Since the Bible gives a much more comprehensive revelation of God than nature, the question of the authorship of the Bible is a vital one. There is much evidence that the Bible is the Word of God. Firstly, the Bible itself teaches that it is the Word of God (2 Timothy 3:16). Secondly, since God has been so directly involved in creating the world, it is consistent that He should reveal the purpose of life in a direct way through the Bible. Thirdly, the Bible has been proved to be very accurate in its statements on history and science. Fourthly, millions of people from all over the world have believed the Bible down through the ages. Fifthly, the Bible has amazing internal consistency. And sixthly, the Bible is the world's oldest book.

God has been very gracious in giving the Bible to mankind because it gives direct answers to the questions of life that cannot be found by simply studying nature. The Bible gives us a communication from God that tells us all we need to know about God, the universe and the purpose of life. It is ironic how governments spend billions of pounds researching evolution and searching for life in space when a detailed account of our origins can be found by simply reading the book of Genesis! It is even more ironic that people who believe in theistic evolution would rather have faith in a man-made and bizarre theory of origins than believe the account of origins that has been directly given to mankind by an infinitely powerful and wise Creator.

Those who do not believe the book of Genesis are not putting their faith in true science but rather in the atheistic beliefs of western society.

The great British scientist Sir Ambrose Flemming who pioneered the development of electronics was strongly opposed to the theory of evolution and he said this about the authenticity of the Bible:

There is abundant evidence that the Bible, though written by man, is not the product of the human mind. By countless multitudes it has always been revered as a communication to us from the Creator of the Universe.[3]

14.3 What is the purpose of life?

Having established that God is our maker and that the Bible is the Word of God, it is now possible to address the question: What is the purpose of life? The Bible declares that people are spiritual beings who are made in the image of God (Genesis 1:27). It also describes how, in the original creation, Adam and Eve enjoyed a close and harmonious relationship with God. In this original creation, the intention was for Adam and Eve to enjoy fellowship with God as well as with one another for eternity in a perfect world. However, after the fall of Adam and Eve, the relationship with God was broken and the natural state of the human being is now one of rebellion against God. This rebellion is very evident in the world today in the way people disregard the Bible and God's commandments. The only way that true joy and peace can be obtained in life is if a person stops being rebellious against God and enters into a relationship with Him. Therefore, the most important purpose in life is to find God and, having found God, to live a life that brings glory to Him. This is why Christian statements of faith often say: 'the chief end of mankind is to glorify God and enjoy Him forever'.

There are many religions that claim to be able to lead a person to God. However, the Bible declares that Jesus Christ is the only way to God (John 14:6). This is because God is perfectly Holy and a person must have their sins forgiven before they can have a relationship with Him. The Bible teaches that only the death of Jesus Christ, God's only Son, is able to pay the penalty for our sins (Ephesians 1:7). The reason why only this sacrifice is acceptable is that the Lord Jesus is the Son of God and lived a perfect sin-free life. No matter how hard we might try, it is impossible for any of us to have our sins forgiven by our own works. The Bible teaches that when a person comes to God through Jesus Christ, they obtain not just peace in this earthly life but they also obtain eternal life.

It is a wonderful thing that the God who created the vast universe is prepared to have communion with individual people. We read about the wonder and joy of this truth in Psalm 8: 'When I consider Your heavens, the work of Your fingers, the moon and the stars, which You have ordained, What is man that You are mindful of him? … You have made him to have dominion over the works of your hands; You have put all things under his feet…O Lord, our Lord, how excellent is Your name in all the earth!' (Psalm 8:3–9).

One of the sad consequences of evolution is that it teaches people that they are not spiritual beings and that the only purpose in life is to get as much sensual enjoyment as possible. This is why the apostle Paul said: '…If the dead do not rise, "Let us eat and drink, for tomorrow we die!"' (1 Corinthians 15:32). Many people firmly believe that the moral decay of society is very strongly linked to the widespread teaching of evolution. Sir Ambrose Flemming said this about the effect of the theory of evolution:

It is disastrous to the ethical development or spiritual life of the young or uneducated to lead them to believe that 'men are descended from monkeys': or that 'the chimpanzee or gorilla are man's nearest relatives.'[4]

Evolution is disastrous because if you teach people that they are animals, then it is inevitable that they will behave like animals.

14.4 What happens after death?

The Bible teaches that our soul will live for eternity, whether or not we come to know God in this life. Therefore, a critical question for everyone is: What happens after death? The Bible teaches that there will be a day of judgement for everyone (Hebrews 9:27). The Bible also teaches that only those who know and trust Jesus Christ will enter into heaven. In one sense, people get what they want when they die. Those people who have ignored God in their earthly life will not know God in the life to come. In contrast, those people who have trusted in the Lord Jesus whilst on earth will enjoy eternal life with God in a perfect heaven.

Some evolutionists claim that the biblical creation account is a myth that has been invented to explain existence. However, it is actually the theory of evolution which is a myth that has been invented to enable people to ignore God. By inventing the myth of evolution, the evolutionist creates a comforting impression that there is no Creator and no Judge. Sadly, for the millions of people who blindly accept the teaching of evolution, such a comfort is false and temporary.

14.5 What will happen to the universe?

According to the theory of evolution, the universe will decay very slowly over billions of years, either by collapsing into a ball of energy or by simply cooling down. Such a future could hardly be more depressing. However, the Bible teaches that God will soon replace this present universe with new heavens and a new earth (Isaiah 65:17). The new creation will be a perfect paradise and God's people will live in it for eternity.

Anyone who finds it difficult to believe that God created the present universe in a supernatural way will surely find it even more difficult to believe that God will supernaturally create new heavens and a new earth. How do theistic evolutionists think God will create the new heavens and new earth? Do they think that He will do it by a process of evolution over millions of years? Such an answer is of course ridiculous but it shows how evolution is inconsistent with the Bible from beginning to end. Those who believe that God created the universe supernaturally as described in Genesis 1 have no difficulty in believing that God will supernaturally create a new and wonderful world to come.

At the beginning of time, God demonstrated great fatherly love in creating a beautiful earth as a home for mankind. Following the sin of Adam and Eve, God showed great mercy and patience in sustaining the world and allowing mankind to fill the earth. God showed His great saving love by sending Jesus Christ, His only Son, to the earth to die on the cross of Calvary for the sins of His people. In the world to come, those who trust in the Creator of the world will see His face and will live with Him for eternity (Revelation 22:4–5).

14.6 The witness of creation

The wonder of creation is spoken of in the book of Job: '...He does great things which we cannot comprehend' (Job 37:5). Modern discoveries have shown that the order and beauty in nature are indeed too great to be comprehended by the human mind. As mankind learns more about the awesome complexities of nature, so the truth of Romans 1:20 becomes ever more apparent, that God's attributes are 'clearly seen' in creation and that the unbeliever is 'without excuse'. In Psalm 14 we read: 'The fool has said in his heart, "There is no God"...' (Psalm 14:1). The Bible commentator Matthew Henry summed up the foolishness of atheism in the following way:

Let us learn hence that atheism is folly, and atheists are the greatest fools in nature, for they see there is a world that could not make itself, and yet they will not own there is a God that made it.[5]

Any reader who believes in evolution is urged to consider the evidence that there is a God who made the world and to seek salvation from this God. In the book of Isaiah God declares His purpose in creation and His ability to save: 'For thus says the Lord, who created the heavens, who is God, who formed the earth and made it, who has established it, who did not create it in vain, who formed it to be inhabited: "I am the Lord, and there is no other ...A just God and a Saviour... Look to Me, and be saved, all you ends of the earth!..."' (Isaiah 45:18–22).

Notes on Chapter 14

1   **Calvin, J.,** *Genesis*, Banner of Truth, Genesis 1:28, p. 105, 1965.

2   **Llewellyn, C.,** *Children's encyclopaedia*, Dorling Kindersley, p. 69, 1997.

3   **Lamont, A.,** *21 Great scientists who believed*, Creation Science Foundation, p. 211, 1995.

4   **Lamont, A.,** *op. cit.*, p. 211.

5   **Henry, M.,** *Bible commentary*, Mac Donald Press, Vol. 3, p. 3, 1710.

Bibliography

The following books are recommended for further reading:

Andrews, E.H., Gitt, W., and **Ouweneel, W.J.,** (Eds), (1986), *Concepts in Creationism*, Evangelical Press, Faverdale North, Darlington, United Kingdom, DL3 0PH.

Beka Educational Text Books:
    History of the World in Christian Perspective
    Science: Order and Reality
    Science: Matter and Motion
    Science of the Physical Creation
    Chemistry: Precision and Design
    Biology: God's Living Creation
    Physics: Foundation Science
    Beka Book Publications, Pensacola Christian College, Box 18000, Pensacola, Florida 32523, USA.
    (All available through Tabernacle Bookshop, Metropolitan Tabernacle, Elephant & Castle, London, SE1 6SD, United Kingdom.)

Burgess Stuart, (2001) *He made the stars also—What the Bible says about the stars,* Day One publications, 3 Epsom Business park, Kiln Lane, Epsom Surrey KT9 2GW

Cooper, W., (1995), *After the Flood: The early post-flood history of Europe traced back to Noah,* New Wine Press, PO Box 17, Chichester, United Kingdom, PO20 6YB.

Gish, D., (1985) *Evolution: the challenge of the fossil record,* Creation life publishers, El Cajon, California, United States of America.

Ham, K., (1988), *The Lie: Evolution,* Master Books, PO Box 26060, Colorado Springs, Colorado, 80936, United States of America.

Bibliography

Ham, K., Snelling, A. and **Wieland, C.,** (1990), *The answers book,* Master Books, PO Box 26060, Colorado Springs, Colorado 80936, United States of America.

Lamont, A., (1995), *21 Great Scientists who believed,* Creation Science Foundation, PO Box 6302, Acacia Ridge D.C., Queensland 4110, Australia.

Lubenow, M.L., (1994), *Bones of Contention: A Creationist Assessment of Human Fossils,* Baker Book House Company, PO Box 6287, Grand Rapids, Michigan, 49516–6287, United States of America.

Masters, P., (1973), *Men of Purpose,* Metropolitan Tabernacle, Elephant & Castle, London, United Kingdom, SE1 6SD.

McIntosh, A., (1997), *Genesis for today,* Day One Publications, 3 Epsom Business Park, Kiln Lane, Epsom, Surrey, United Kingdom, KT17 1JF.

Monty White, A.J., (1978), *What about Origins,* Dunestone Printers Ltd., 43, Gestridge Road, Kinsteignton, Newton Abbot, Devon, United Kingdom, TQ12 3EZ.

Morris, H.M. and **Parker, G.E.,** (1987), *What is Creation Science?,* Master Books, PO Box 26060, Colorado Springs, Colorado, 80936, United States of America.

Morris, H.M., *The Genesis Record,* Baker Book House, Grand Rapids, Michigan, 49516, United States of America.

Morris, H.M., (1988), *Science and the Bible,* Scripture Press, Amersham-on-the Hill, Buckinghamshire, United Kingdom HP6 6JK.

Morris, H.M., (1982), *Men of Science—Men of God,* Master Books, PO Box 26060, Colorado Springs, Colorado, 80936, United States of America.

Morris, J.D., (1994), *The Young Earth,* Master Books, PO Box 26060, Colorado Springs, Colorado, 80936, United States of America.

Pink, A.W., (1975), *The attributes of God,* Baker Book House, Grand Rapids, Michigan 49516, United States of America.

Powell, E., (1999), *On Giants' Shoulders,* Day One Publications, 3 Epsom Business Park, Kiln Lane, Epsom, Surrey, United Kingdom, KT17 1JF.

Rosevear, D., (1991), *Creation Science—confirming that the Bible is right,* New Wine Press, PO Box 17, Chichester, United Kingdom, PO20 6YB.

Spetner, L., (1997), *Not by Chance,* The Judaica Press, Brooklyn, New York, United States of America.

Sutherland, L.D., (1988), *Darwin's Enigma: Fossils and other Problems,* Master Books, California, United States of America.

Watson, David C.C., (1975), *The Great Brain Robbery—Studies in Evolution,* Henry E. Walter Ltd, Worthing, Sussex, United Kingdom.

Watson, David C.C., (1976), *Myths and Miracles—A new approach to Genesis 1–11,* Henry Walter Ltd, 26, Grafton Road, Worthing, Sussex, United Kingdom.

Whitcomb, J.C. and **Morris, H.M.,** (1969), *The Genesis Flood—The Biblical Record and its Scientific Implications,* Evangelical Press, Faverdale North, Darlington, United Kingdom, DL3 0PH.

Whitcomb, J.C., (1972), *The early earth,* Evangelical Press, Faverdale North, Darlington, United Kingdom, DL3 0PH.

Whitcomb, J.C., (1973), *The world that perished,* Evangelical Press, Faverdale North, Darlington, United Kingdom, DL3 0PH.

Wieland, C., (1994), *Stones and Bones,* Creation Science Foundation, PO Box 6302, Acacia Ridge, Queensland 4110, Australia.

Wilder-Smith, A.E., (1981), *The Natural Sciences know nothing of evolution,* Master Books, PO Box 26060, Colorado Springs, Colorado, 80936, United States of America.

Creation Organisations

Biblical Creation Society, PO Box 22, Rugby, Warwickshire, United Kingdom, CV22 7SY. Magazine *Origins* produced 4 times a year.
Web-page: http://www.pages.org/bcs

Answers in Genesis (UK), (Creation Science Foundation (UK)), 147 Queen's Road, Leicester, United Kingdom, LE2 3FL, telephone: (0116) 2708400, fax: (0116) 2700110.
Web-page: http://www.answersingenesis.org/uk

Creation Science Movement, PO Box 888, Portsmouth, United Kingdom, PO6 2YD. Newsletter produced monthly with regular articles.
Web-page: http://www.creationsciencemovement.com

Creation Resources Trust, PO Box 3237, Yeovil, United Kingdom, BA22 7WD, telephone or fax: 01935 850569. Regular children's broadsheet, *Our World* produced. Student's broadsheet, '*Original View* and newsletter approx. 4 times a year.
Web-page: http://www.c-r-t.co.uk

Index

Also by the same author

What the Bible says about the stars

STUART BURGESS

192 PAGES

£6.99

US $11.99

CAN $13.99

1 903087 13 9

There is a great need for a book which gives clear biblical teaching on the purpose of the stars and the question of extraterrestrial life. This book meets that need. The book starts by showing how the earth has a unique purpose of supporting life and that the stars have a unique purpose of shining light on the earth. It then shows how modern-day discoveries in astronomy about the earth and its position in the Universe have demonstrated the astounding truth of this biblical teaching. The book also describes why the Universe contains outstanding natural beauty and how the stars reveal the glory, power, wisdom and goodness of God. The final sections of the book deal with the topical question of whether there is extraterrestrial life in space. The book gives a historical overview of man's belief and describes some of the major projects that are being carried out to search for life in space. It shows that from biblical doctrines on creation and salvation, there can be no possibility of any alien life in space. The book presents many fascinating facts about the Universe in an easy-to-understand style. Illustrated.

REFERENCE: HMS

He made the stars also

What the Bible says about the stars

Stuart Burgess

"Both our world and the heavens seem to sparkle with a new identity as a consequence of this book"
— REV GEOFF THOMAS

Day One

'Dr Burgess has a very clear style and his book brims with interesting material. It will be greatly appreciated'

DR PETER MASTERS, METROPOLITAN TABERNACLE